CHRISTMAS AT KING'S COLLEGE

CAROLS, HYMNS AND SEASONAL ANTHEMS FOR MIXED VOICES FROM THE CHOIR OF KING'S COLLEGE, CAMBRIDGE

SELECTED BY STEPHEN CLEOBURY

NOVELLO

NOV040073
ISBN: 978-1-84938-267-0

Project management by Elizabeth Robinson
Music setting by Chris Hinkins
Cover design by Ruth Keating

Cover image of King's College Chapel by Emma Disley
Back cover images:
Portrait of Stephen Cleobury © Simon Fowler
Kings College Chapel Vaulted Ceiling by Colin D. Young/istockphoto.com

Published in Great Britain by Novello Publishing Limited
(Part of The Music Sales Group)

Head office:
14-15, Berners Street,
London W1T 3LJ, UK

Tel: +44 (0)20 7612 7400
Fax: +44 (0)20 7612 7549

Sales and hire:
Music Sales Distribution Centre
Newmarket Road
Bury St. Edmunds
Suffolk IP33 3YB, UK

Tel: +44 (0)1284 702600
Fax: +44 (0)1284 768301

www.chesternovello.com

Contents

trad. arr. Stephen Cleobury Once in royal David's city 1
Praetorius, arr. James Whitbourn A great and mighty wonder 4
Otto Goldschmidt A tender shoot 10
trad. arr. Stephen Cleobury A virgin most pure 12
Philip Ledger Adam lay ybounden 23
Peter Wishart Alleluya, a new work is come on hand 27
John Tavener Away in a manger 37
Stephen Cleobury Be merry 42
Peter Warlock Benedicamus Domino 49
Peter Sculthorpe The birthday of thy King 53
Arvo Pärt Bogoroditsye Dyevo 60
Diana Burrell Christo paremus cantica 62
trad. arr. David Willcocks God rest you merry, gentlemen 73
trad. arr. Stephen Cleobury Good King Wenceslas 76
trad. arr. Simon Preston I saw three ships come sailing in 84
Carl Rütti I wonder as I wander 92
Patrick Hadley I sing of a maiden 96
Judith Weir Illuminare, Jerusalem 99
Lennox Berkeley In wintertime 105
trad. arr. Stephen Cleobury Infant holy, infant lowly (W żłobie leży) 110
trad. arr. David Willcocks The Infant King 116
trad. arr. Stephen Cleobury It came upon the midnight clear 118
Elizabeth Poston Jesus Christ the apple tree 122
John Tavener The Lamb 124
Peter Sculthorpe Morning song for the Christ Child 128
R. R. Terry Myn lyking 132
Paul Edwards No small wonder 134
R. O. Morris Love came down at Christmas 139
French trad. arr. Stephen Jackson Noël nouvelet 140
Richard Rodney Bennett Nowel 153
trad. arr. Vaughan Williams The truth sent from above 159
trad. arr. Vaughan Williams O little town of Bethlehem (I) 160
Henry Walford Davies O little town of Bethlehem (II) 164
trad. arr. Stephen Cleobury Of the Father's heart begotten 168
trad. arr. Philip Ledger On Christmas night all Christians sing (The Sussex Carol) 173
trad. arr. Stephen Cleobury Šai svētā naktī (On this holy night) 178
J. F. Wade arr. Stephen Cleobury O come, all ye faithful 188
Bob Chilcott The shepherd's carol 193
Franz Gruber arr. Cleobury Silent night (2009 setting) 199
trad. arr. Roxanna Panufnik Sleep, little Jesus, sleep 204
trad. arr. Stephen Cleobury Suo Gân 211
Jonathan Dove The three Kings 216
John Rutter What sweeter music 230
John Joubert When Christ was born of Mary free 238
trad. arr. Stephen Cleobury While shepherds watched their flocks by night 244
Mendelssohn arr. Stephen Cleobury Hark! the herald angels sing 246
Readings and repertoire for *A Festival of Nine Lessons and Carols* 250

Preface

A Festival of Nine Lessons and Carols was first celebrated in the Chapel of King's College, Cambridge in 1918. Based upon a liturgical scheme devised by Bishop Benson for Truro in 1880, its fixed sequence of scriptural readings moves from the account of the fall in Genesis, through the Old Testament prophecies of the coming of Christ, to the Gospel accounts of the birth of the Saviour and of some of the *dramatis personae* involved, the Shepherds and the Wise Men, culminating in St John's unfolding of 'the great mystery of the Incarnation'. The progress of the narrative is punctuated by carols and hymns, the choice of which varies from year to year, inspired by, and reflecting upon, these very well known biblical passages, still today read in the King James version.

The carol repertory is vast, ranging from the medieval corpus through the nineteenth century revival, to the vibrant and exciting contemporary scene, in which the quantity and variety of new compositions and arrangements refutes any notion that this is a fossilised tradition. At the same time. the current rise in the popularity of choral singing is a real encouragement to composers.

In planning this anthology, I have kept in mind the principles which have guided my own selections for the annual Festival for each Christmas Eve since 1982. Broadly speaking, the aim is to present a mixture of old and new, familiar and less familiar, allowing a long and hallowed tradition to be both respected as we look back and to be developed and refreshed as we look forward.

Many of the old favourites are here and fall comfortably within the range of most choirs. Some of them are in traditional arrangements, some in new versions. Practically everything has been performed on radio or television during my time as Director of Music, and has a King's or Cambridge connection. Of particular interest, I hope, will be those carols which have been commissioned by the College annually since 1982: a tradition which continues. In 2005, EMI released a CD *On Christmas Day*, which featured the King's Choir in twenty-two of these special commissions.

For reasons of space, some frequently anthologised 'King's' carols have had to give way to less easily available material, but it has been a particular pleasure to include items by my two immediate predecessors, Sir David Willcocks and Sir Philip Ledger, to whom King's and I personally owe so much. We have included some of my own arrangements (and a newly composed piece, *Be Merry*) and I have taken the opportunity to write fresh arrangements of a number of well-known hymns. A feature of these which may appeal to choirs is that the final verses allow the singers to maintain four-part harmony: while the descant, naturally, remains in the soprano part, the melody appears in one or more of the other parts. They are designed in such a way, however, that they can be performed with just descant and unison melody, the organ always providing the full harmony.

Stephen Cleobury, Director of Music
King's College, Cambridge, 2009

Once in royal David's city

C.F. Alexander (1818–95)

H.J. Gauntlett (1805–76)
harmonised by A.H. Mann (1850–1929)
verse 6 arr. Stephen Cleobury (b.1948)

v. 6 overleaf

3. And through all his wondrous childhood
He would honour and obey,
Love and watch the lowly maiden,
In whose gentle arms he lay:
Christian children all must be
Mild, obedient, good as he.

4. For he is our childhood's pattern,
Day by day like us he grew,
He was little, weak, and helpless,
Tears and smiles like us he knew:
And he feeleth for our sadness,
And he shareth in our gladness.

5. And our eyes at last shall see him,
Through his own redeeming love,
For that child so dear and gentle
Is our Lord in heaven above;
And he leads his children on
To the place where he is gone.

*6. Not in that poor lowly stable,
With the oxen standing by,
We shall see him; but in heaven,
Set at God's right hand on high;
When like stars his children crowned
All in white shall wait around.

* Verse 1 may be sung by a solo treble/soprano.
** Verse 6 words provided here for congregational use only.

S.
13
6. Not in that poor low - ly__ sta - ble, With__ the__
A.
6. Not in that poor low - ly__ sta - ble, With the
T.
6. Not in that poor low - ly sta - ble, With the__
B.
6. Not in that poor low - ly sta - ble, With the
15
ox - en stand - ing__ by, We shall see him; but in__
ox - en stand - ing__ by, We shall see him; but__ in__
ox - en stand - ing__ by,__ We shall see him; but in
ox - en stand - ing by,__ We shall see him; but in

18
hea - ven, Set at God's right hand on high; When like
hea - ven, Set at God's right hand on high; When like
hea - ven, Set at God's right hand on high; When like
hea - ven, Set at God's right hand on high; When like
21
stars his child - ren crowned All in white shall wait a - round.
stars his child - ren crowned All in white shall wait a - round.
stars his child - ren crowned All in white shall wait a - round.
stars his child - ren crowned All in white shall wait a - round.

A great and mighty wonder

St Germanus (634–c.733)
tr. J.M. Neale
(1818–66)

M. Praetorius (1571–1621)
arr. James Whitbourn (b.1963)

SOPRANO *f*
A great and migh-ty won - der, A full and ho - ly cure. The

ALTO *f*
A great and migh-ty won - der, A full and ho - ly cure. The

TENOR *f*
A great and migh-ty won - der, A full__ and ho - ly cure. The

BASS *f*
A great and migh-ty won - der, A full and ho - ly cure. The

PIANO
(for rehearsal only)

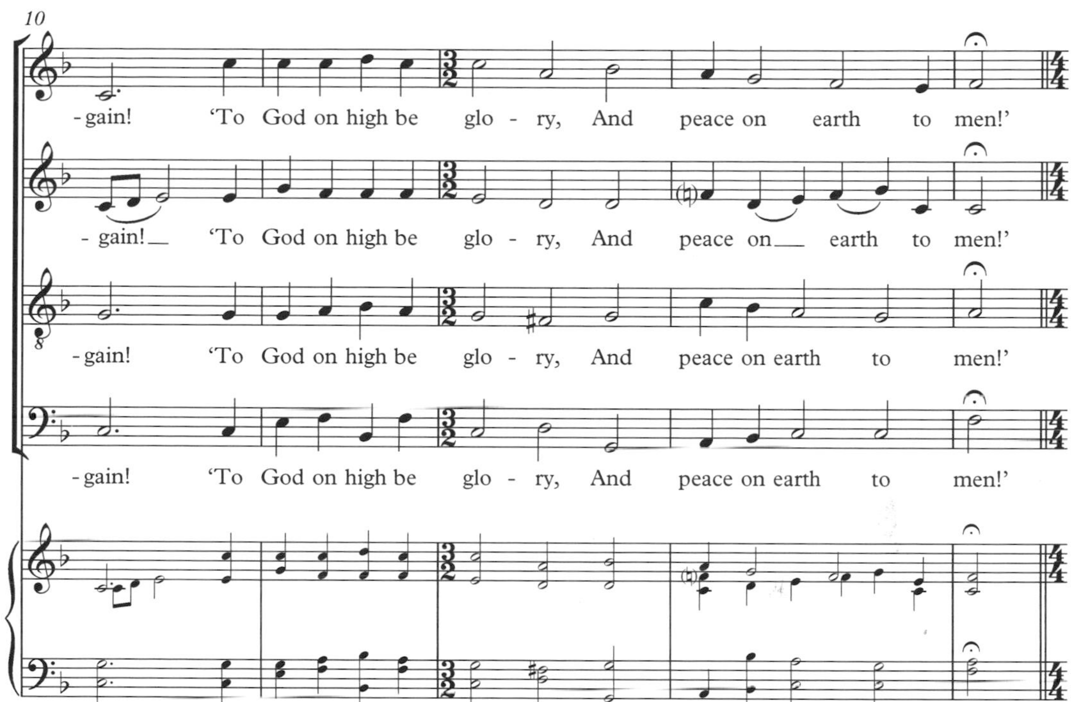
10
-gain! 'To God on high be glo - ry, And peace on earth to men!'
-gain! 'To God on high be glo - ry, And peace on earth to men!'
-gain! 'To God on high be glo - ry, And peace on earth to men!'
-gain! 'To God on high be glo - ry, And peace on earth to men!'

15
mf
And
mf
And
mf
2. The Word be-comes in - car - nate And yet re - mains on high.
mf
2. The Word be-comes in - car - nate And yet re - mains on high.

19
f
che-ru-bim sing an-thems To shep-herds from the sky. Re-peat the hymn a-
che-ru-bim sing an-thems To shep-herds from the sky. Re-peat the hymn a-
Re-peat the hymn a-
Re-peat the hymn a-

24
-gain! 'To God on high be glo - ry, And peace on earth to men!'
-gain! 'To God on high be glo - ry, And peace on earth to men!'
-gain! 'To God on high be glo - ry, And peace on earth to men!'
-gain! 'To God on high be glo - ry, And peace on earth to men!'

S. p
29
3. While thus they sing your mon - arch, Those bright an - ge - lic
A. p
3. While thus they sing your mon - arch, Those bright an - ge - lic
32
S.
bands,
A.
bands,
TENOR mf
Re - joice, ye vales and moun - tains, Ye o - ceans clap your
BASS mf
Re - joice, ye vales and moun - tains, Ye o - ceans clap your
36
f
Re - peat the hymn a - gain! 'To God on high be glo - ry, And
f
Re - peat the hymn a - gain! 'To God on high be glo - ry, And
hands. Re - peat the hymn a - gain! 'To God on high be glo - ry, And
hands. Re - peat the hymn a - gain! 'To God on high be glo - ry, And

41
ff
peace on earth to men!' 4. Since all he comes to
peace on earth to men!' 4. Since all he comes to
peace on earth to men!' 4. Since all he comes to
peace on earth to men!' 4. Since all he comes to
44
ran - som, By all be he a - dored, The in - fant born in
ran - som, By all be he a - dored, The in - fant born in
ran - som, By all be he a - dored, The in - fant born in
ran - som, By all be he a - dored, The in - fant born in
ran - som, By all be he a - dored, The in - fant born in

48
Beth - l'em The Sav - iour and the Lord. Re - peat the hymn a -
Beth - l'em The Sav - iour and the Lord. Re - peat the hymn a -
Beth - l'em The Sav - iour and the Lord. Re - peat the hymn a -
Beth - l'em The Sav - iour and the Lord. Re - peat the hymn a -
Beth - l'em The Sav - iour and the Lord. Re - peat the hymn a -
52
mf
dim.
p
- gain! 'To God on high be glo - ry, And peace on earth to men!'
- gain! 'To God on high be glo - ry, And peace on earth to men!'
- gain! 'To God on high be glo - ry, And peace on earth to men!'
- gain! 'To God on high be glo - ry, And peace on earth to men!'

A tender shoot

Otto Goldschmidt
tr. William Bartholomew (1793–1867)

Otto Goldschmidt
(1829–1907)

9
f
blooms with-out a blight, it blooms with - out a blight,
God of end - less might, our God of end - less might
blooms with-out a blight, with - out a blight,
God of end - less might, of end - less might
blooms with-out a blight, it blooms with - out a blight,
God of end - less might, our God of end - less might
blooms with-out a blight, it blooms with - out a blight,
God of end - less might, our God of end - less might
13
rall. a tempo rit.
pesante
fz più p pp
blooms in the cold bleak win - ter turn - ing our dark - ness in - to light.
gave her this child to save us, thus turn-ing dark - ness in - to light.
blooms in the cold bleak win - ter turn - ing our dark - ness in - to light.
gave her this child to save us, thus turn-ing dark - ness in - to light.
blooms in the cold bleak win - ter turn - ing our dark - ness in - to light.
gave her this child to save us, thus turn-ing dark - ness in - to light.
blooms in the cold bleak win - ter turn - ing our dark - ness in - to light.
gave her this child to save us, thus turn-ing dark - ness in - to light.
rall. a tempo rit.

A virgin most pure

English traditional
arr. Stephen Cleobury

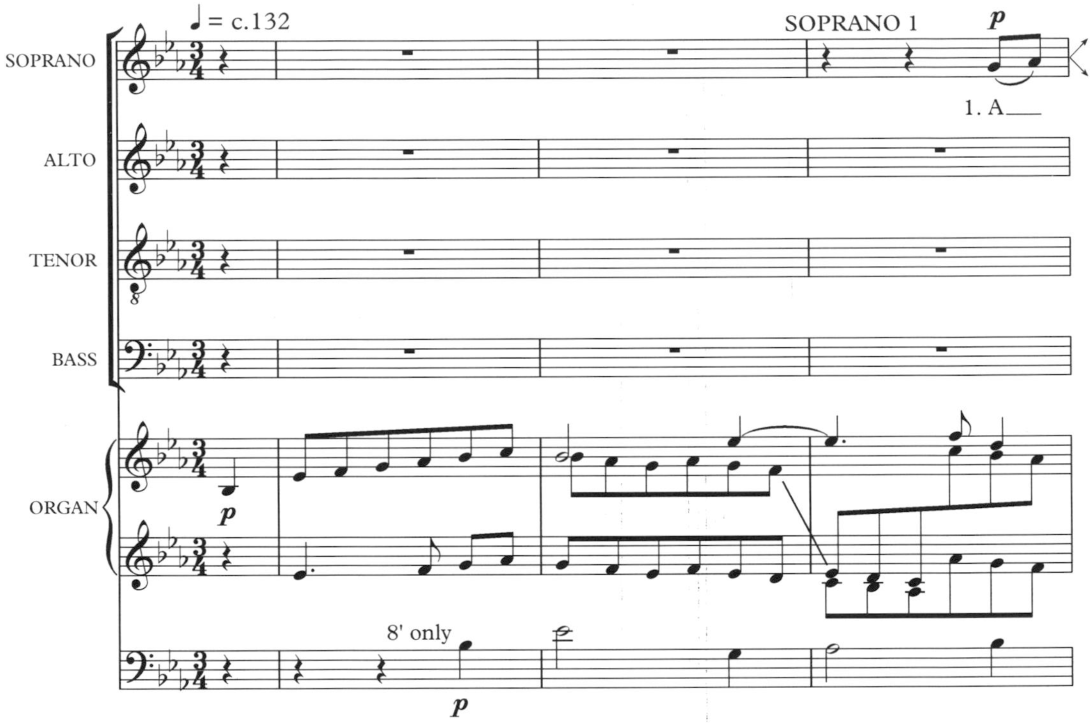

♩ = c.132
SOPRANO
ALTO
TENOR
BASS
ORGAN
SOPRANO 1
p
1. A
p
8' only
p

4
S.1
vir - gin most pure as the pro - phets do tell, Hath brought forth a
SOPRANO 2
p
Hath brought forth a

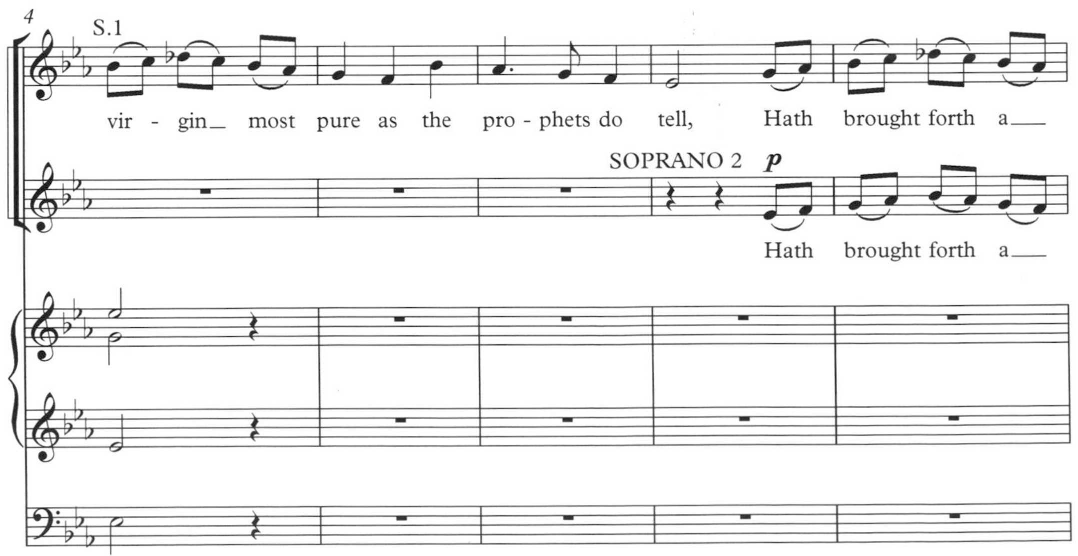

9
S.1
ba - by as it hath be - fell, To be our Re -
S.2
ba - by as it hath_ be - fell, To be our Re -
ALTO p
Re -
TENOR p
Re -
(BASS)

13
- deem - er from death, hell_ and sin, Which A - dam's trans -
-deem - er from death, hell_ and sin,_ Which A - dam's trans -
-deem - er from death, hell and sin, Which A - dam's trans -

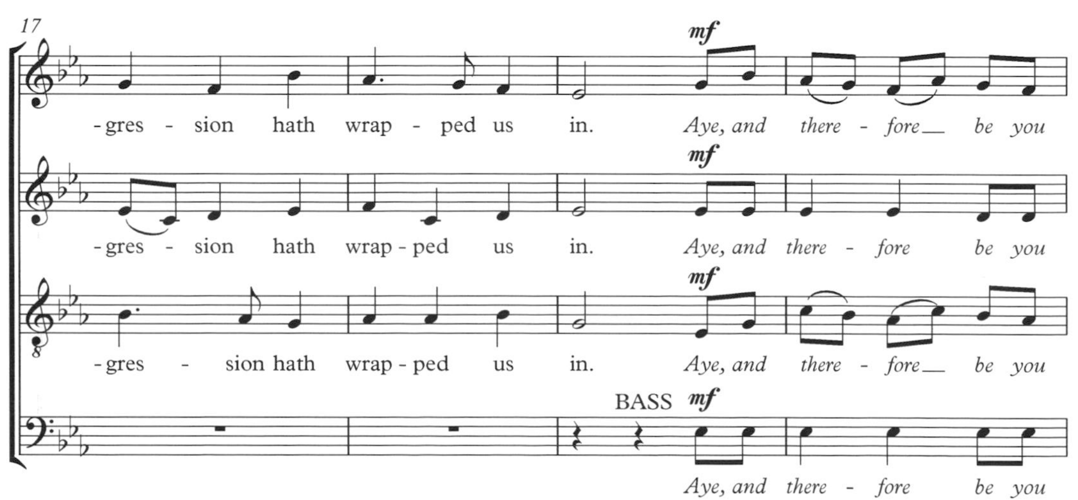
17
mf
- gres - sion hath wrap - ped us in. Aye, and there - fore_ be you
mf
- gres - sion hath wrap - ped us in. Aye, and there - fore be you
mf
- gres - sion hath wrap - ped us in. Aye, and there - fore_ be you
BASS mf
Aye, and there - fore be you

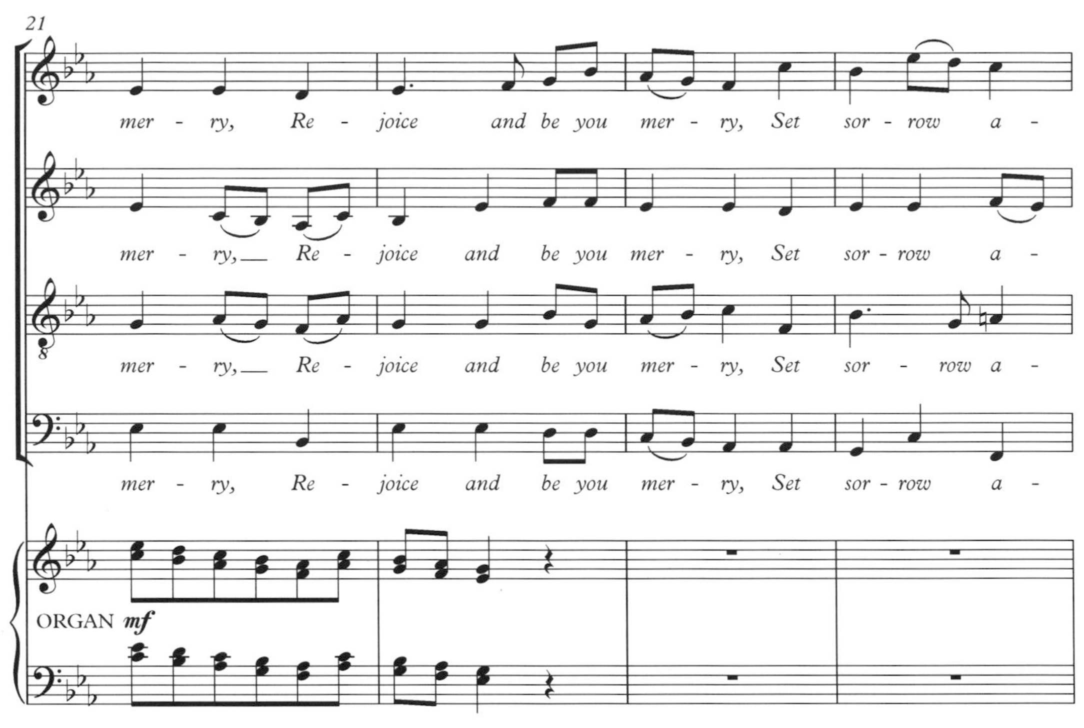

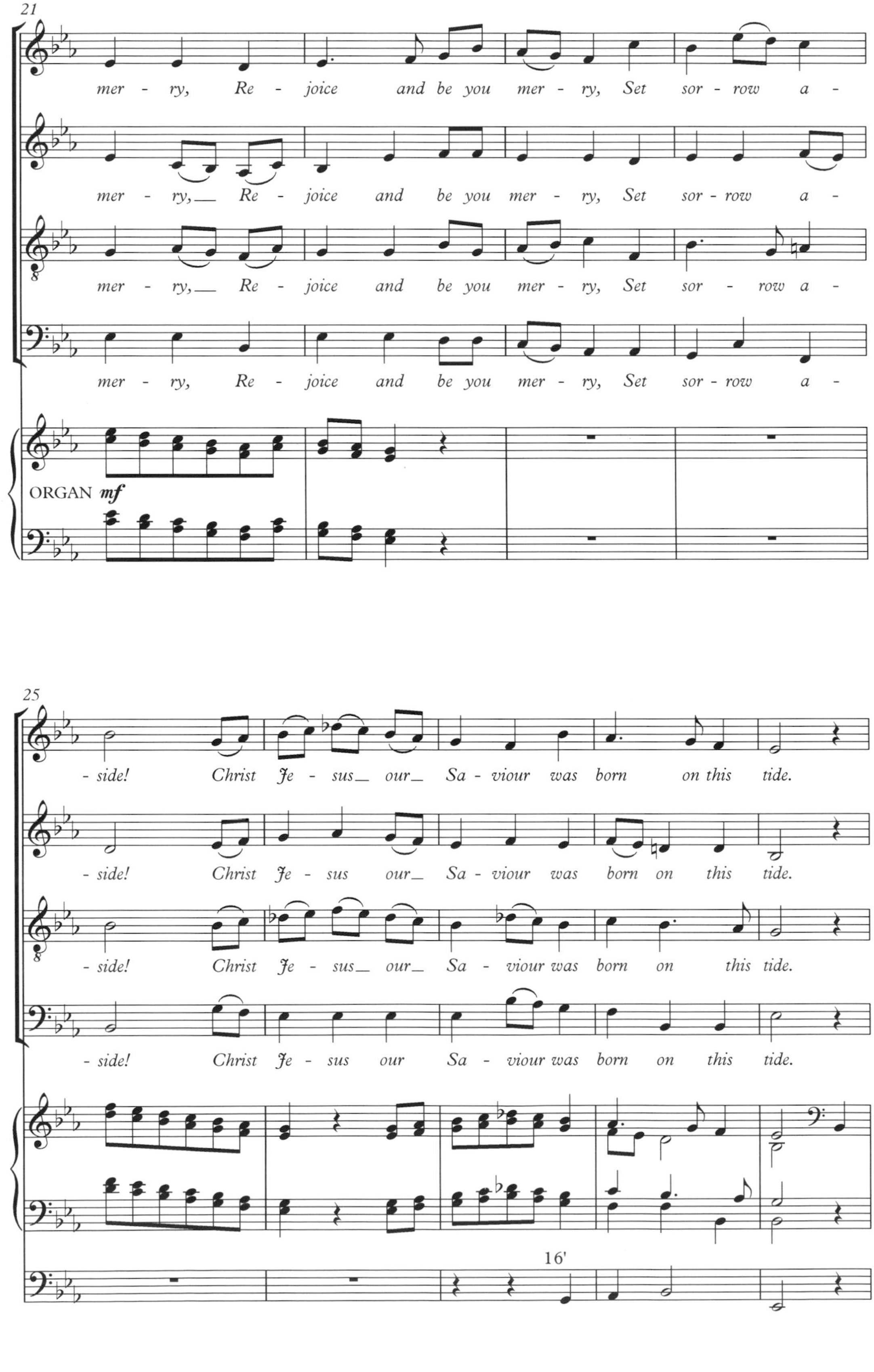
21
mer - ry, Re - joice and be you mer - ry, Set sor - row a -
mer - ry, Re - joice and be you mer - ry, Set sor - row a -
mer - ry, Re - joice and be you mer - ry, Set sor - row a -
mer - ry, Re - joice and be you mer - ry, Set sor - row a -
ORGAN mf
25
- side! Christ Je - sus our Sa - viour was born on this tide.
- side! Christ Je - sus our Sa - viour was born on this tide.
- side! Christ Je - sus our Sa - viour was born on this tide.
- side! Christ Je - sus our Sa - viour was born on this tide.
16'

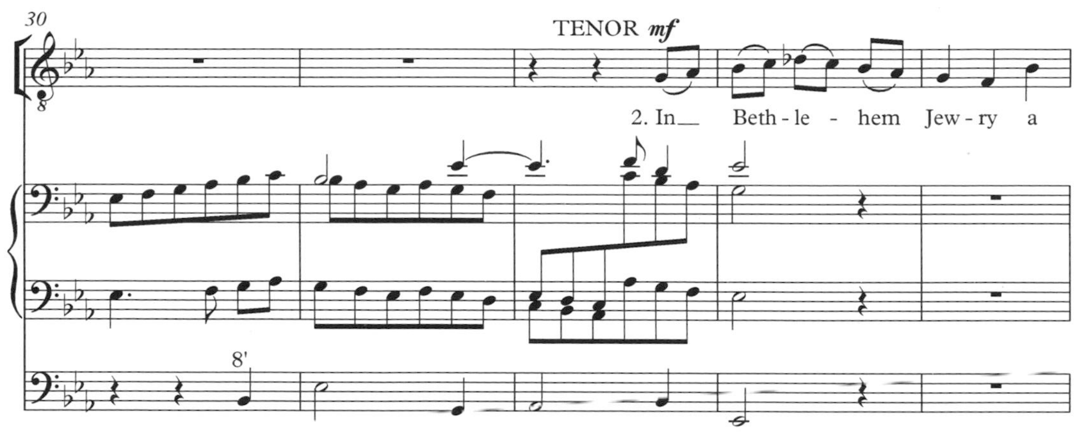
30
TENOR mf
2. In Beth - le - hem Jew - ry a
8'

35
ci - ty there was, Where Jo - seph and Ma - ry to - ge - ther did
BASS 1 mf
Where Jo - seph and Ma - ry to - ge - ther did

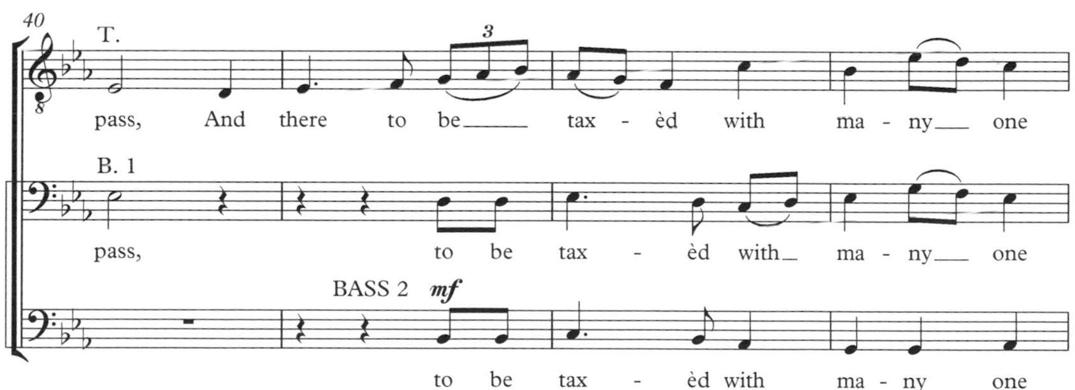
40
T.
pass, And there to be tax - èd with ma - ny one
B. 1
pass, to be tax - èd with ma - ny one
BASS 2 mf
to be tax - èd with ma - ny one

44
mo', For Cae - sar com - mand - ed the same should be
mo', For Cae - sar com - mand - ed the same should be
mo', For Cae - sar com - mand - ed the same should be

48
SOPRANO
Aye, and there - fore be you mer - ry, Re - joice and be you
ALTO
Aye, and there - fore be you mer - ry, Re - joice and be you
T.
so. Aye, and there - fore be you mer - ry, Re - joice and be you
B.
so. Aye, and there - fore be you mer - ry, Re - joice and be you

52
mer - ry, Set sor - row a - side! Christ Je - sus our
mer - ry, Set sor - row a - side! Christ Je - sus our
mer - ry, Set sor - row a - side! Christ Je - sus our
mer - ry, Set sor - row a - side! Christ Je - sus our

56
mf cresc.
Sa - viour was born on this tide. 3. But_ when they had_
Sa - viour was born on this tide.
mf
Sa - viour was born on this tide. they
mf
Sa - viour was born on this tide. they
mf
16'
61
f
en - tered the ci - ty so fair, The_ num - ber_ of_
mf cresc.
f
the ci - ty so fair, The_ num - ber_ of_
cresc.
f
en - tered the ci - ty so fair, The_ num - ber_ of_
cresc.
f
en - tered the ci - ty so fair,_ The_ num - ber_ of_
mf

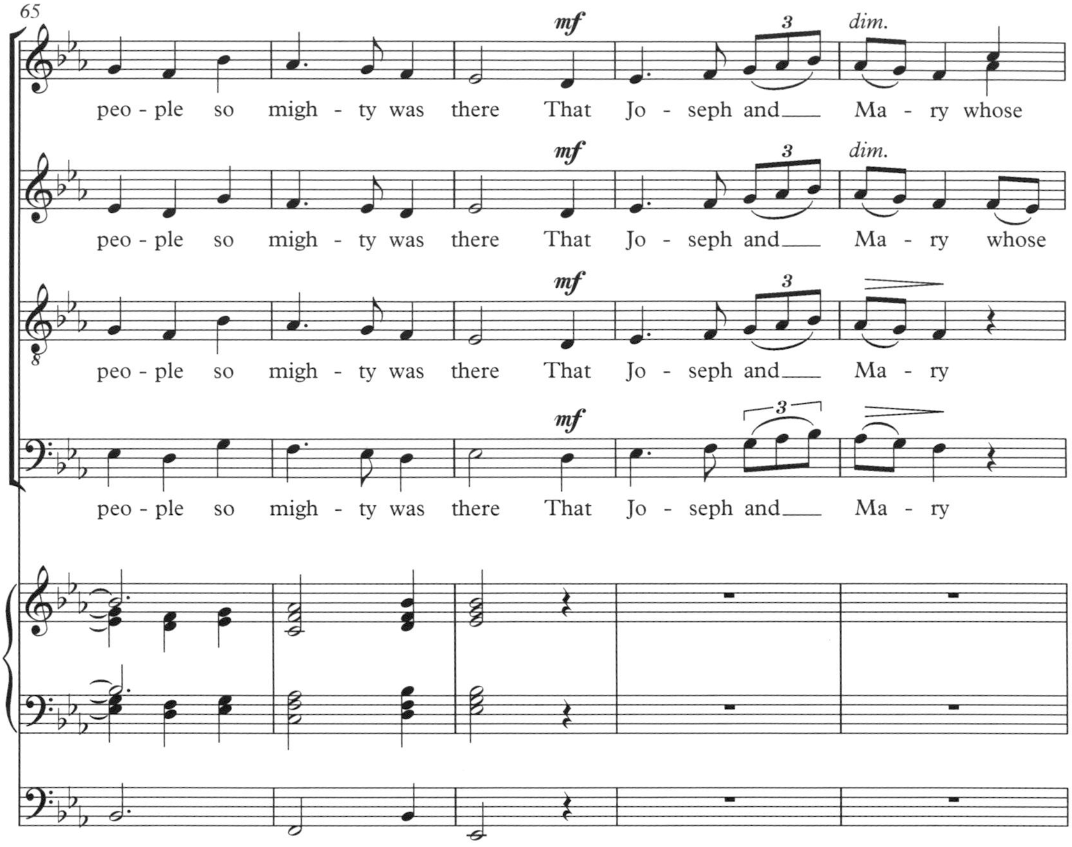

65

mf 3 *dim.*

peo - ple so migh - ty was there That Jo - seph and Ma - ry whose

mf 3 *dim.*

peo - ple so migh - ty was there That Jo - seph and Ma - ry whose

mf 3

peo - ple so migh - ty was there That Jo - seph and Ma - ry

mf 3

peo - ple so migh - ty was there That Jo - seph and Ma - ry

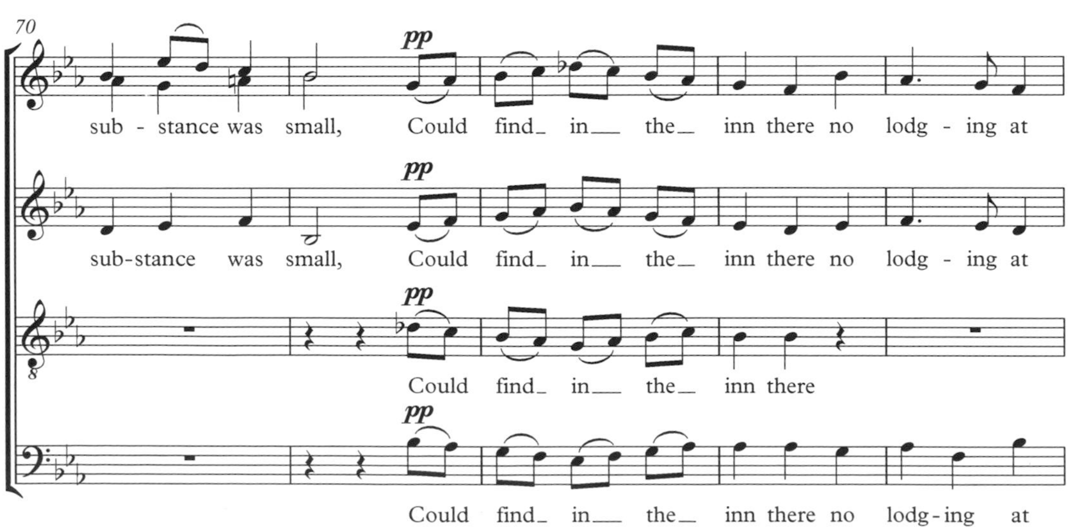

75
p
all. Aye, and there - fore be you mer - ry, Re - joice and be you
all. Aye, and there - fore be you mer - ry, Re - joice and be you
Aye, and there - fore be you mer - ry, Re - joice and be you
all. Aye, and there - fore be you mer - ry, Re - joice and be you

79
mer - ry, Set sor - row a - side! Christ Je - sus our
mer - ry, Set sor - row a - side! Christ Je - sus our
mer - ry, Set sor - row a - side! Christ Je - sus our
mer - ry, Set sor - row a - side! Christ Je - sus our

83
Sa - viour was born on this tide.
Sa - viour was born on this tide.
Sa - viour was born on this tide. 4. Then
Sa - viour was born on this tide. 4. Then
mp

87

were_ they_ con - strained in a sta - ble to lie, Where

were_ they_ con - strained in a sta - ble to lie, Where

mp

91

mp cresc.

3

Their lodg - ing so___

hor - ses_ and_ as - ses they used for to tie;

hor - ses_ and_ as - ses they used for to tie;

96
poco f
simple they took it no scorn, But against the next
mf
took it no scorn, But against the next
But against the next
But against the next
100
f
morn-ing our Sa-viour was born. Be mer-ry, Re-
morn-ing our Sa-viour was born. Be mer-ry, Re-
morn-ing our Sa-viour was born. Aye, and there-fore be you mer-ry, Re-
morn-ing our Sa-viour was born. Aye, and there-fore be you mer-ry, Re-

105
-joice, be mer - ry, Set sor - row a - side! Christ
-joice and be you mer - ry, Set sor - row a - side! Christ
-joice and be you mer - ry, Set sor - row a - side! Christ
-joice and be you mer - ry, Set sor - row a - side! Christ
109
Je - sus our Sa - viour was born on this tide.
Je - sus our Sa - viour was born on this tide.
Je - sus our Sa - viour was born on this tide.
Je - sus our Sa - viour was born on this tide.

for Mary

Adam lay ybounden

15th century

Philip Ledger (b.1937)

13

mf cantabile

— 2. And all was for an ap - ple, An ap - ple that he took, As clerk - es

mf

— As clerk - es

mf

- *as!* As clerk - es

- *as!*

19

find - en Writ - ten in their book. *p* *De - o*, — *De - o*, — *De - o graci-*

find - en Writ - ten in their book. *p* *De - o*, — *De - o*, — *De - o graci-*

find - en Writ - ten in their book. *p* —

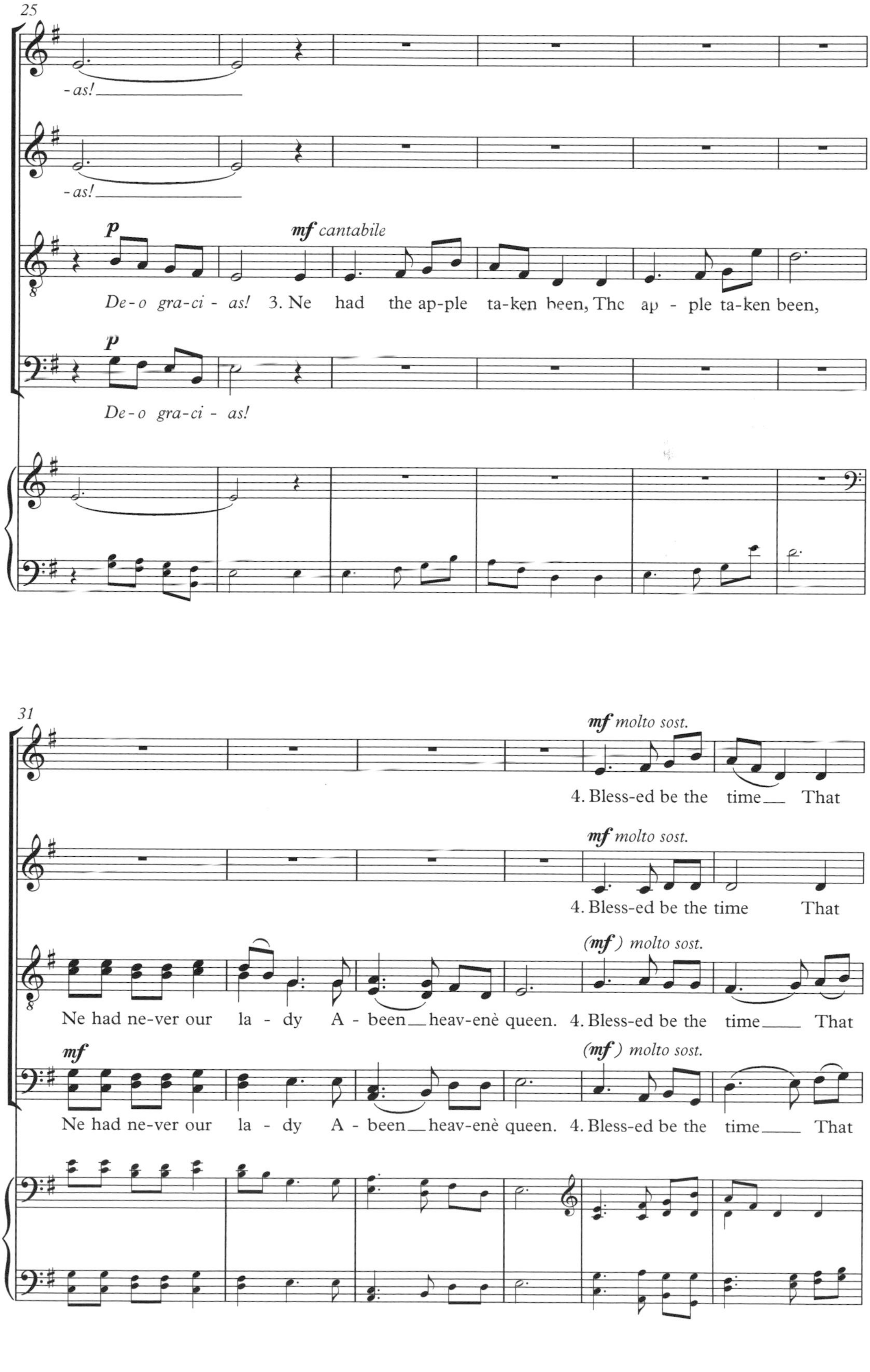

25

-as!

-as!

p **mf** *cantabile*

De-o gra-ci - as! 3. Ne had the ap-ple ta-ken been, The ap - ple ta-ken been,

p

De-o gra-ci - as!

37

f

ap - ple ta-ken was, There-fore we moun sing - en *De - o gra - ci -*

f

ap - ple ta-ken was, There-fore we moun sing - en *De - o gra - ci -*

f

ap - ple ta-ken was, There-fore we moun sing - en *De - o gra - ci -*

f

ap - ple ta-ken was, There-fore we moun sing - en *De - o gra - ci -*

42

p pp

- as! De - o, De - o, De-o gra-ci - as!

p pp

- as! De - o, De - o, De-o gra-ci - as!

p pp

- as! De - o gra - ci - as!

p pp

- as! De - o gra - ci - as!

for the Birmingham Singers' Club

Alleluya, a new work is come on hand

15th century

Peter Wishart
(1921–84)

from *Three Carols* by Peter Wishart

4
-ya, al - le - lu - ya, al - le - lu ya, al - le - lu - ya,
al - le - lu - ya, al - le - lu - ya, al - le - lu - ya,
-ya, al - le - lu - ya, al - le - lu ya, al - le - lu - ya,
al - le - lu - ya, al - le - lu - ya, al - le - lu - ya,
-ya, al - le - lu - ya,
-ya, al - le - lu - ya,
7
al - le - lu - ya. 1. A new work is come on hand
al - le - lu - ya. 1. A new work is come on hand
al - le - lu - ya. 1. A new work is come on hand Through
al - le - lu - ya. 1. A new work is come on hand Through

11
Through might and grace of God's Son
Through might and grace of God's Son
mf
might and grace of God-e's Son To save the lost of ev-'ry
mf
might and grace of God-e's Son To save the lost of ev-'ry
14
p f f
Al - le - lu-ya, For now is free that erst was
Al - le-lu - ya, al-le - lu - ya, For now is free that erst was
Al - le - lu-ya, For now is free that erst was
Al - le-lu - ya, al-le - lu - ya, For now is free that erst was
land. Al-le-lu-ya, For now is free that erst was
land. Al-le-lu-ya, For now is free that erst was

18
bound; We may well sing
Al - le - lu -
Al - le - lu - ya,
Al - le - lu -
22
- ya, al - le - lu - ya, al - le - lu ya, al - le - lu - ya,
al - le - lu - ya, al - le - lu - ya, al - le - lu - ya,
- ya, al - le - lu - ya, al - le - lu - ya.

25
al - le - lu - ya.
2. Now is ful-fill-èd the pro-phe-cy
al - le - lu - ya.
2. Now is ful-fill-èd the pro-phe-cy
al - le - lu - ya.
2. Now is ful-filled the pro-phe - cy
Of
al - le - lu - ya.
2. Now is ful-filled the pro-phe - cy
Of

29
Of Da-vid and Je - re - my
Of Da-vid and Je - re - my
Da - vid and of Je - re - my
And al - so of I - sai -
Da - vid and of Je - re - my
And al - so of I - sai -

32
Al - le - lu - ya, Sing
Al - le - lu - ya, al - le - lu - ya, Sing
Al - le - lu - ya, Sing
Al - le - lu - ya, al - le - lu - ya, Sing
-ah; Al - le - lu - ya, Sing
-ah; Al - le - lu - ya, Sing
35
we there-fore both loud and high, both loud and high:
we there-fore both loud and high, both loud and high:
we there-fore both loud and high, both loud and high:
we there-fore both loud and high, both loud and high:

39
Al - le-lu - ya, al - le-lu - ya, al - le-lu -
Al - le-lu-ya, al - le-lu-ya, al - le-lu-ya,
Al - le-lu - ya, al - le-lu - ya, al - le-lu -
Al - le-lu-ya, al - le-lu-ya, al - le-lu-ya,
Al - le - lu - ya, al - le-lu -
Al - le - lu - ya, al - le-lu -
42
-ya, al - le - lu - ya, al - le - lu - ya.
al - le - lu - ya, al - le - lu - ya.
-ya, al - le - lu - ya, al - le - lu - ya.
al - le - lu - ya, al - le - lu - ya.
f
-ya. al - le - lu - ya. 3. Al -
f
-ya. al - le - lu - ya. 3. Al -

45
f
3. Al - le - lu- ya, this swee-té song
f
3. Al - le - lu- ya, this swee-té song
-le - lu - ya this swee-té song
Out of a green branch it
-le - lu - ya this swee-té song
Out of a green branch it
48
mf
Out of a green branch it sprung.
Al -
mf
Out of a green branch it sprung.
Al - le - lu -
mf
Out of a green branch it sprung.
Al -
mf
Out of a green branch it sprung.
Al - le - lu -
mf
sprung.
God send us the life that last-eth long!
mf
sprung.
God send us the life that last-eth long!

51
Poco meno allegro e pesante
f
-le - lu - ya,
Now joy and bliss be him a -
-ya, al - le - lu - ya,
Now joy and bliss be him a -
-le - lu - ya,
Now joy and bliss be him a -
-ya, al - le - lu - ya,
Now joy and bliss be him a -
Al - le - lu - ya,
Now joy and bliss be him a -
Al - le - lu - ya,
Now joy and bliss be him a -
Poco meno allegro e pesante
54
-mong
That thus
can sing
-mong
That thus
can sing
-mong
That thus
can sing
-mong
That thus
can sing

57
a tempo
Al - le - lu - ya, al - le - lu - ya, al - le - lu -
Al - le - lu - ya, al - le - lu - ya, al - le - lu - ya,
Al - le - lu - ya, al - le - lu - ya, al - le - lu -
Al - le - lu - ya, al - le - lu - ya, al - le - lu - ya,
Al - le - lu - ya, al - le - lu -
Al - le - lu - ya, al - le - lu -
a tempo
60
ff
-ya, al - le - lu - ya, al - le - lu - ya.
al - le - lu - ya, al - le - lu - ya.
-ya, al - le - lu - ya, al - le - lu - ya.
al - le - lu - ya, al - le - lu - ya.
- ya, al - le - lu - ya.
- ya, al - le - lu - ya.

Commissioned by King's College, Cambridge, 2005
to Theodora and Sofia

Away in a manger

American 19th century

John Tavener
(b.1944)

11
p
bright sky looked down where he lay, The lit - tle Lord Je - sus a - sleep
bright sky looked down where he lay, The lit - tle Lord Je - sus a - sleep
bright sky looked down where he lay, The lit - tle Lord Je - sus a - sleep
bright sky looked down where he lay, The lit - tle Lord Je - sus a - sleep
17
Very strong
p molto f
on the hay. 2. The cat - tle are low - ing, the ba - by a -
on the hay. 2. The cat - tle are low - ing, the ba - by a -
on the hay. 2. The cat - tle are low - ing, the ba - by a -
on the hay. 2. The cat - tle are low - ing, the ba - by a -
Very strong

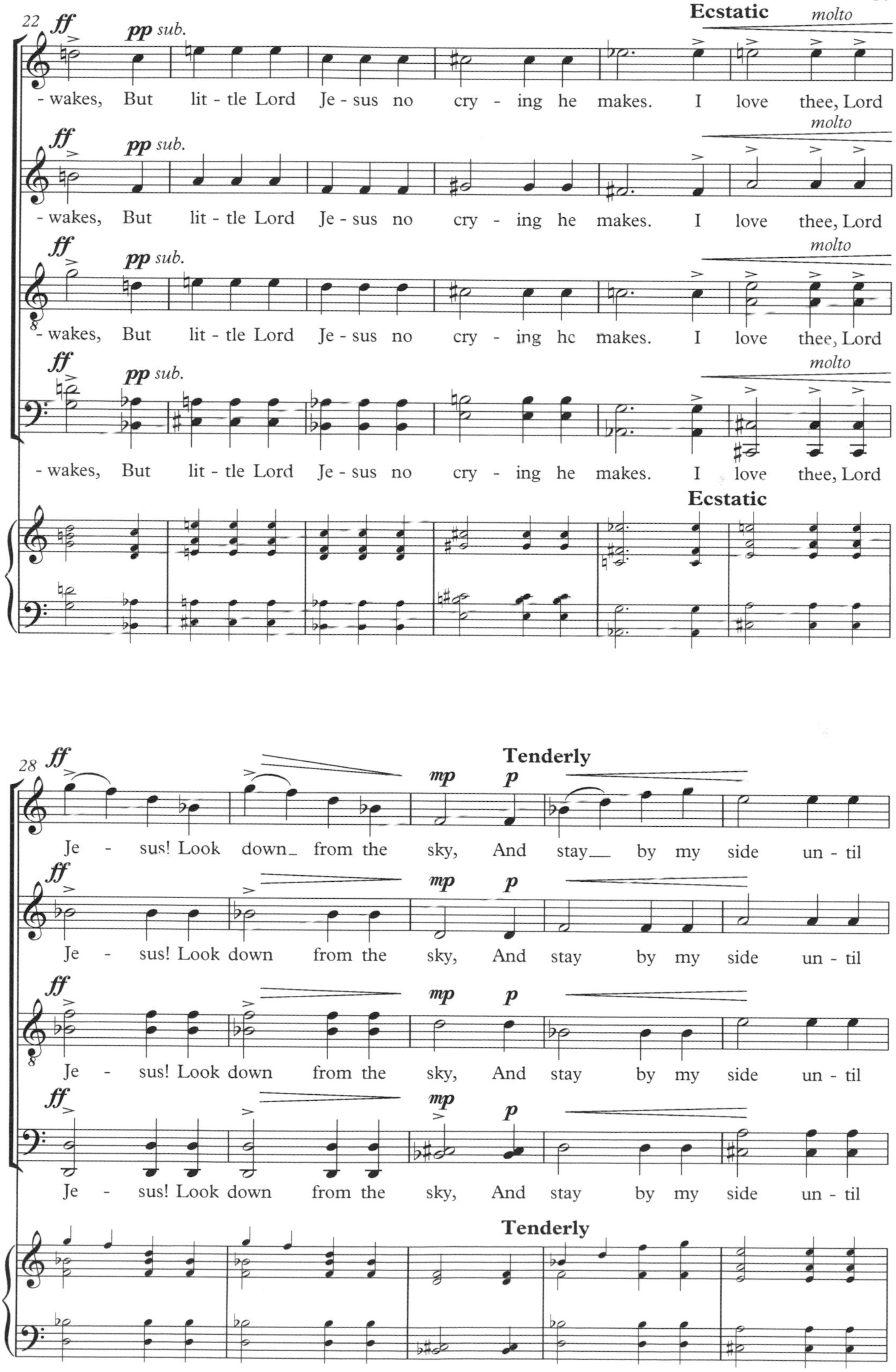

22

Ecstatic *molto*

-wakes, But lit-tle Lord Je-sus no cry-ing he makes. I love thee, Lord

28

Tenderly

Je-sus! Look down from the sky, And stay by my side un-til

rit. . . . . **Rapt, lost in wonder and prayer** (♩ = c.52)

33

SOPRANO SOLO

p

3. Be near me, Lord

espress.

morn - - - - ing is nigh. *p* *pp humming* *Mm*

espress.

morn - - - - ing is nigh. *p* *pp humming* *Mm*

espress.

morn - - - - ing is nigh. *p* *pp humming* *Mm*

espress.

morn - - - - ing is nigh. *p* *pp humming* *Mm*

rit. . . . . **Rapt, lost in wonder and prayer** (♩ = c.52)

38

Je - sus; I ask thee to stay Close by me for e - ver, and love me, I

mm *mm*

mm *mm*

mm *mm*

mm *mm*

44

pray. ______ Bless all the dear__ child - ren in thy ten - der

mm ______

mm ______

mm ______

mm ______

49

rit.

care, And fit us for hea - ven, to live ____ with thee there.

mm ______

mm ______

mm ______

mm ______

rit.

Manor Farm House
25th December 2004

Commssioned by the Worshipful Company of Musicians in 2004
for the Company's annual carol service at St. Michael's Church, Cornhill, London

to Emma

Be merry

c.1440

Stephen Cleobury

9
S.
Tutti
f
cha - ri - ty, It is mer - ry to be In Him that is but One. Be
ALTO f
Be

14
S.
mer-ry, be mer-ry, I pray you, be mer-ry ev' - ry one.
A.1
mer ry, be mer-ry, I pray you, be mer-ry ev' - ry one.
A.2
mer-ry, be mer-ry, I pray you, be mer-ry ev' - ry one.
Man. f

18
TENOR mf
2. For He that is but One in bliss To us hath sent His son, y wis, To

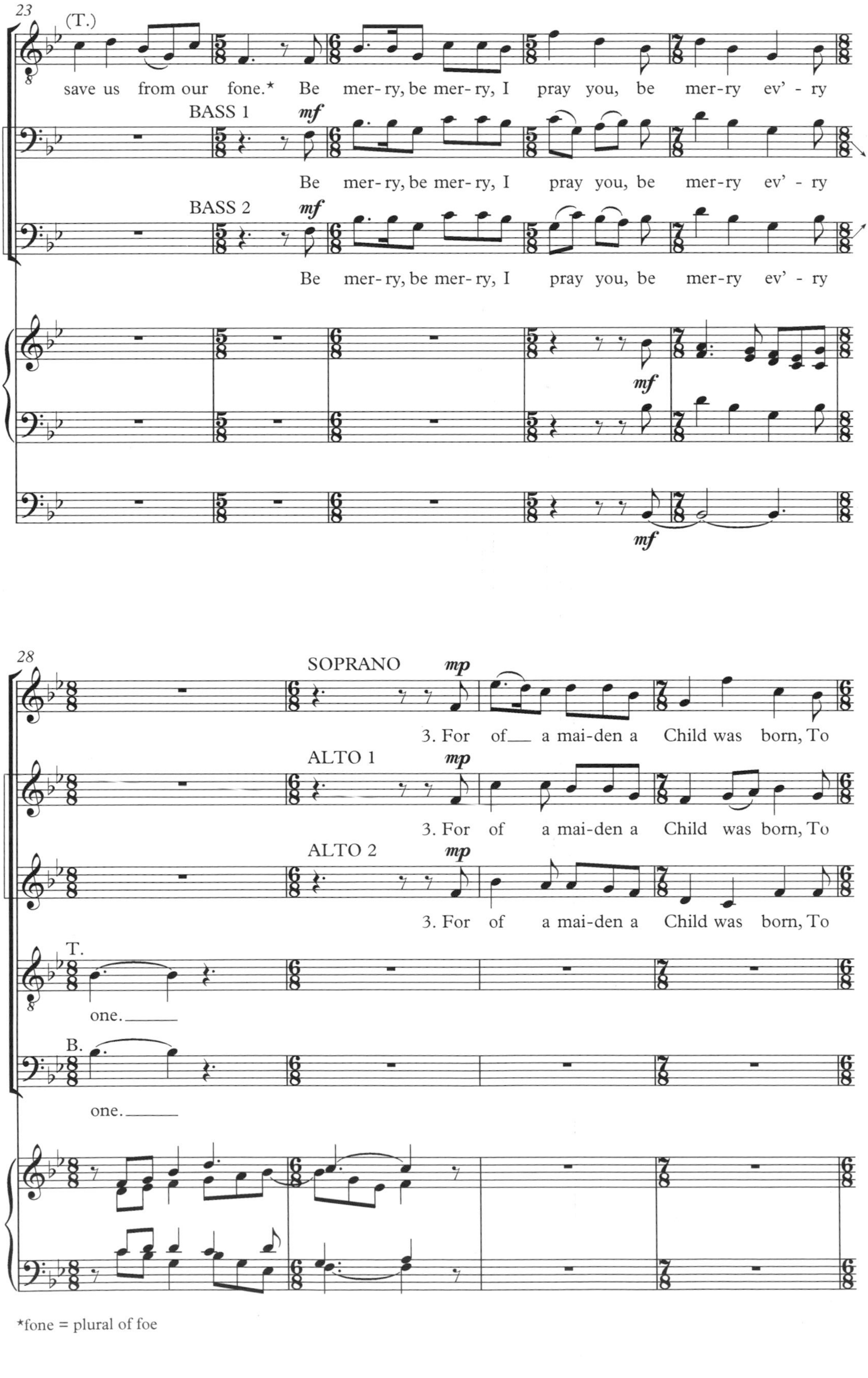

28

SOPRANO mp

3. For of a mai-den a Child was born, To

ALTO 1 mp

3. For of a mai-den a Child was born, To

ALTO 2 mp

3. For of a mai-den a Child was born, To

T.

one.

B.

one.

*fone = plural of foe

32
save man - kind that was for - lorn. Man think there - on. Be
save man - kind that was for - lorn. Man think there - on. Be
save man-kind that was for - lorn. Man think there - on. Be
Be
Be
36
mer- ry, be mer- ry, I pray you, be mer - ry ev' - ry one.
mer- ry, be mer- ry, I pray you, be mer - ry ev' - ry one.
mer- ry, be mer- ry, I pray you, be mer - ry ev' - ry one.
mer- ry, be mer- ry, I pray you, be mer - ry ev' - ry one.

40
mf
4. Now Ma - ry, for thy Son His sake, Save them all that
B. 1
mf
4. Now Ma - ry, for thy Son His sake, Save them all that
B. 2
mf
4. Now Ma - ry, for thy Son His sake, Save them all that
44
mf
Be mer - ry, be mer - ry, I
mf
Be mer - ry, be mer - ry, I
mirth do make, And hold the long - est on. Be mer - ry, be mer - ry, I
mirth do make, And hold the long - est on. Be mer - ry, be mer - ry, I
mirth do make, And hold the long-est on. Be mer - ry, be mer - ry, I

48
pray you, be mer - ry ev' - ry one, Be mer - ry ev' - ry
pray you, Be mer - ry ev' - ry one, Be
pray you, be mer - ry ev' - ry one, Be mer - ry ev' - ry
pray you, Be mer - ry ev' - ry one, Be
pray you, be mer - ry ev' - ry one, Be mer - ry ev' - ry
pray you, Be mer - ry ev' - ry one, Be
pray you, be mer - ry ev' - ry one, Be mer - ry ev' - ry
pray you, Be mer - ry ev' - ry one, Be

52
ff
one,
ev'-ry one.
mer - ry ev' - ry one,
ev'-ry one.
one,
ev'-ry one.
mer - ry ev' - ry one,
ev'-ry one.
one,
ev'-ry one.
mer - ry ev' - ry one,
ev'-ry one.
one,
ev'-ry one.
mer - ry ev' - ry one,
ev'-ry one.

Benedicamus Domino

Sloane MS. 2593 (15th century)

Peter Warlock
(1894–1930)

12

mf *mp*

E - ya, no-bis an-nus est! Na-tus est de vir - gi-ne

mf *mp*

E - ya, no-bis an-nus est! Na-tus est de vir - gi-ne

mf *mp*

E - ya, no-bis an-nus est! Na-tus est de vir - gi-ne

mf *mp*

Si-ne vi-ri se-mi-ni E - ya, no-bis an-nus est! Na-tus est de vir - gi-ne

18

f

Glo - ri - a! Lau - des! De-us ho-mo fac-tus est et im-mor - tal - lis.

f

Glo - ri - a! Lau - des! De - us ho-mo fac - tus est et im-mor - tal - lis.

f

Glo - ri - a! Lau - des! De-us ho-mo fac-tus est et im-mor - ta - lis.

f *p*

Glo - ri - a! Lau - des! De-us ho-mo fac - tus est et im-mor - tal - lis. *Ah*

23

mp Si-ne vi-ri co-pi-a E-ya no-bis an-nus est! *mp* Na-tus est ex Ma-ri-a

mp Si-ne vi-ri co-pi-a E-ya no-bis an-nus est! *mp* Na-tus est ex Ma-ri-a

mp E-ya no-bis an-nus est! *mp* Na-tus est ex Ma-ri-a

mp Na-tus est ex Ma-ri-a

29

f Glo-ri-a! Lau-des! De-us ho-mo fac-tus est et im-mor-tal-lis. *f risoluto* In

f Glo-ri-a! Lau-des! De-us ho-mo fac-tus est et im-mor-tal-lis. *f risoluto* In

f Glo-ri-a! Lau-des! De-us ho-mo fac-tus est et im-mor-tal-lis. *f risoluto* In

f Glo-ri-a! Lau-des! De-us ho-mo fac-tus est et im-mor-tal-lis. *f risoluto* In

With the boy-child's coming forth
Joy! For us the promised time!
Coming forth from the Virgin's womb
Glory and Praise Be!
God made man and yet undying.

Not of human generation
He is born of a virgin:
Not of human machination
He is born of Mary:
In this endless holy day
We do bless the Lord!

for the Choir of King's College, Cambridge

The birthday of thy King

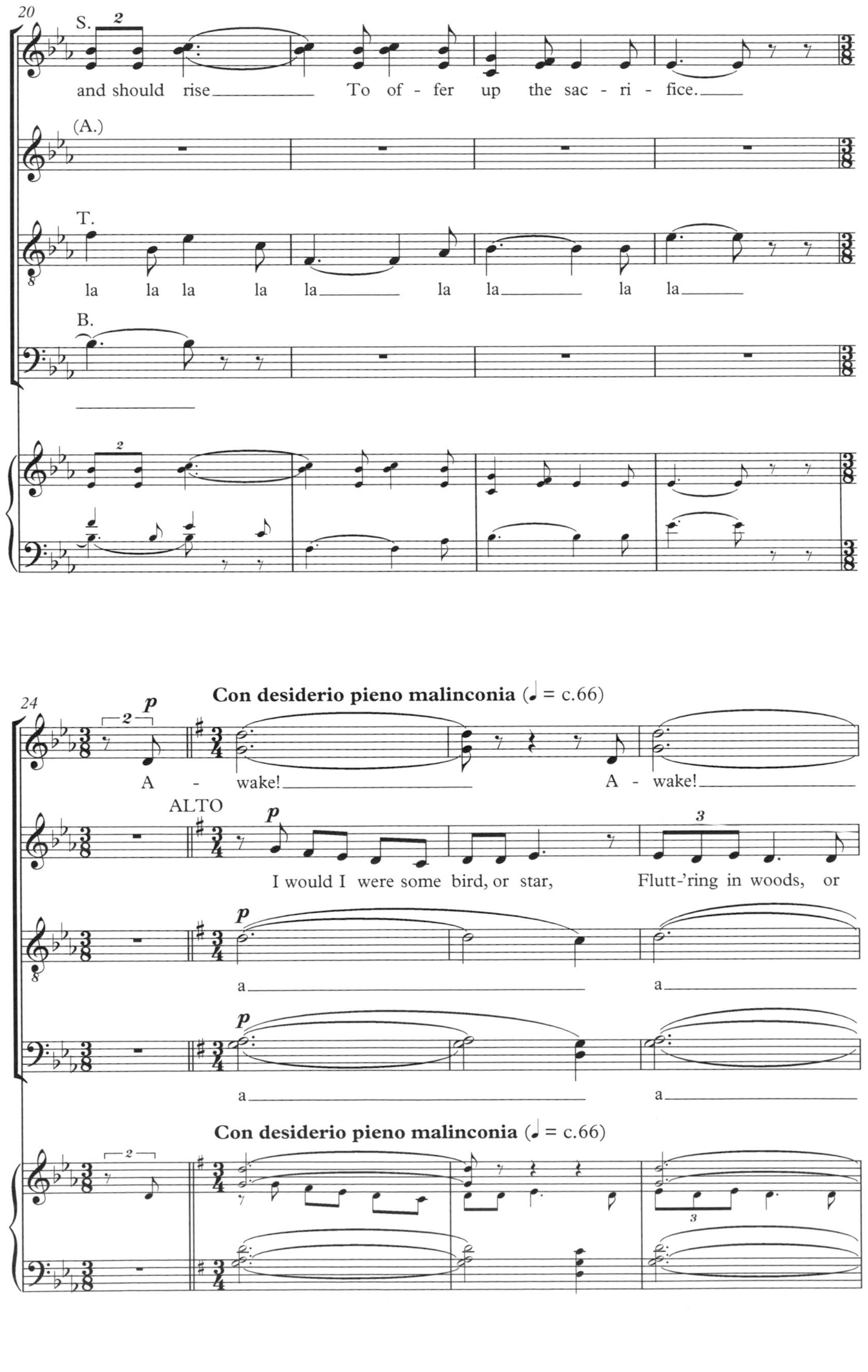

24

Con desiderio pieno malinconia (♩ = c.66)

S. *p*
A - wake! A - wake!

ALTO *p*
I would I were some bird, or star, Flutt-'ring in woods, or

T. *p*
a a

B. *p*
a a

Con desiderio pieno malinconia (♩ = c.66)

28
mp
A - wake!
lift - ed far A - bove this inn And road of sin; Then ei - ther star or
a a a
a a a
32
lunga
mf
A - wake! A - wake!
bird should be Shin - ing or sing - ing still to Thee. I would I had in
a a
a a

36
f
A - wake! A
my best part Fit rooms for Thee! Or that my heart Were so clean as Thy man-ger was!
a a a
a a a
41
p
- wake! A - wake! Sweet
f
But I am all filth, and ob- scene; And on-ly Thou canst make me clean.
f
a a
f
a a

45
Meno mosso
lunga
Je - su! Will then, will then. A-
a a
p sub.
a Let no more This le-per haunt and soil Thy door!
a Let no more This le-per haunt and soil Thy door!
Meno mosso
49
Giubilante (♩. = c.76)
S.
-wake, glad heart! Get up, and sing! It is the birth - day
ALTO
Sweet Je - su!
Giubilante (♩. = c.76)
52
of thy King. A - wake! A-wake! The sun doth shake Light from his locks, and
Sweet Je - su!

56
all the way
Breath - ing
per - fumes, doth spice the
day.
Je - su!
60
S.
(f)
A - wake! A - wake!
How the wood rings!
Whis - per - ing winds and
A.
f
Sweet
Je - su!
TENOR f
La la la la la la la la la la la la la
BASS
f
A - wake!
64
bu - sy springs
A
con - cert make; A - wake! A - wake!
Man is their high priest,
Sweet
Je - su!
la la la la la la la la la la la la la la la la
A - wake!

68

and should rise ____ To of - fer up the sac - ri - fice. ____

____ Je - su! ____

la la la la la ____ la la ____ la la ____

____

72

Meno mosso

p Sweet ____ *mf* Je - su. ____

mf Je - su. ____

mf Je - su. ____

p Sweet *mf* Je - su. ____

Meno mosso

to Stephen Cleobury and King's College Choir, Cambridge

Bogoroditsye Dyevo

(*Mother of God and Virgin*)

Words from the Liturgy of Vespers

Arvo Pärt (b. 1935)

Rejoice, O virgin Mary, full of grace, the Lord is with thee:
blessed art thou among women, and blessed is the fruit of thy womb,
for thou hast borne the Saviour of our souls.

23
ff
ya - ko Spa - sa ro - dee - la ye - see doosh na - shikh.
(rehearsal only)
26
p sub.
Bo-go - ro-dee-tse Dye-vo ra-dui-sya, Bla-go-dat-na-ya Ma - ree-ye Go-
32
-spod s To - bo - yu; Bla-go-slo-vye-na Ti v zhe-nakh ee bla-go-slo-vyen plod
37
Più lento
rit.
chrye-va Tvo-ye - go, ya-ko Spa-sa ro-dee-la ye - see doosh na - shikh.

for Stephen Cleobury and the Choir of King's College, Cambridge. Christmas Eve, 1993

Christo paremus cantica

15th century

Diana Burrell (b.1948)

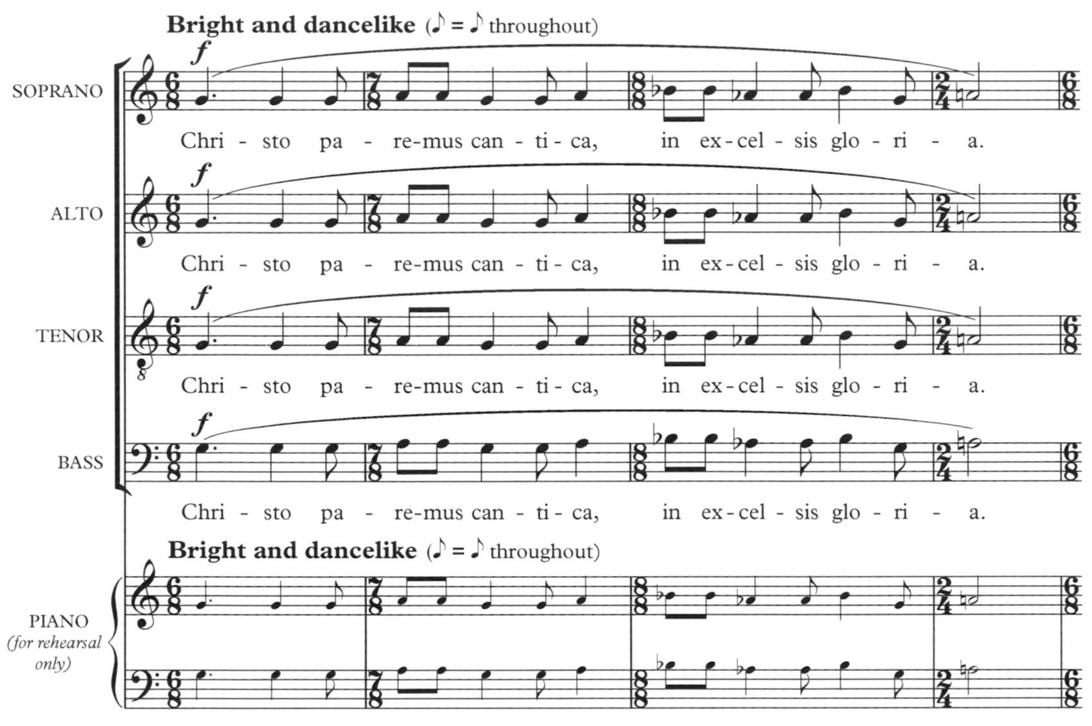

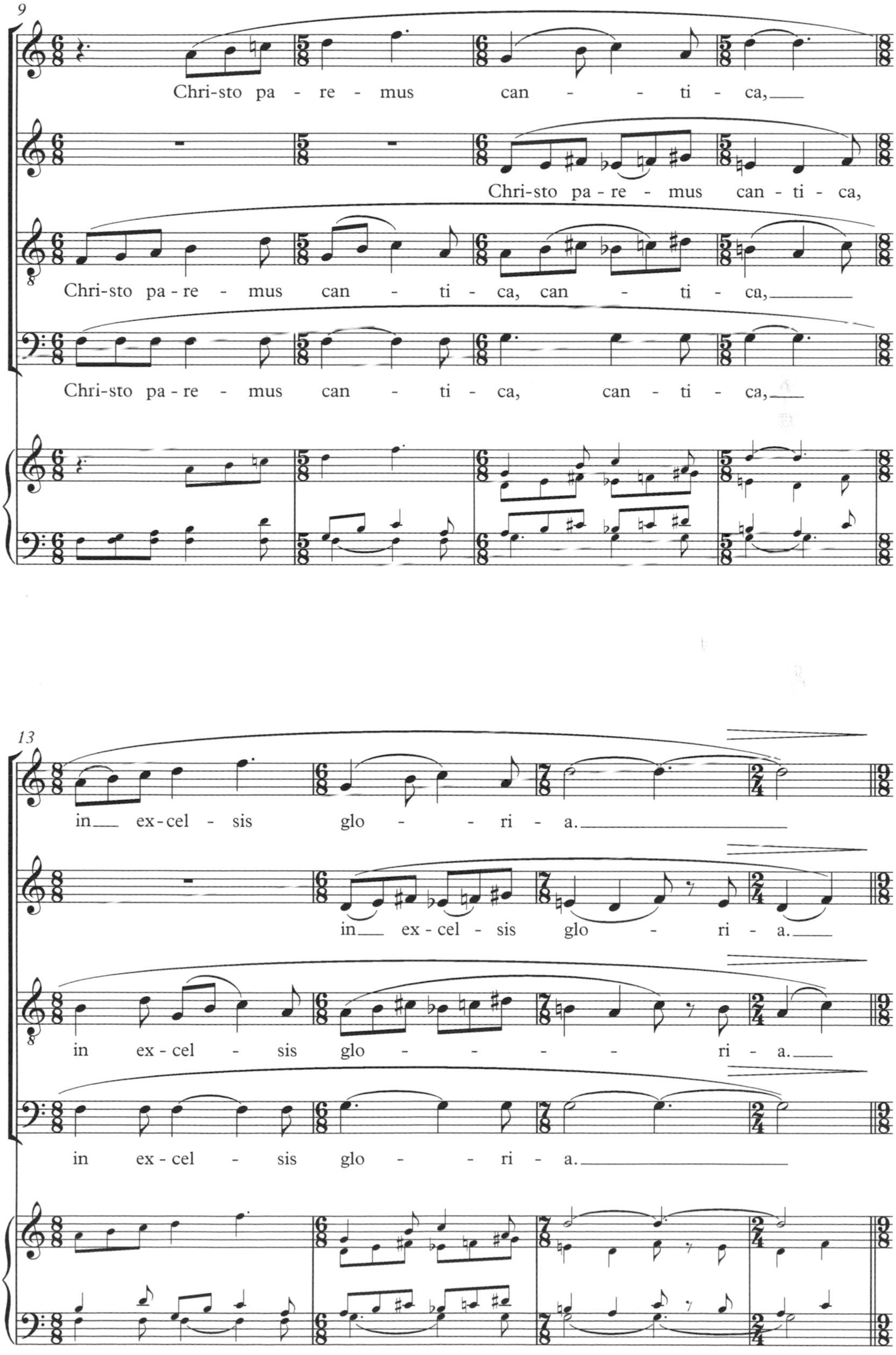

13
in ex-cel - sis glo - - ri - a.
in ex - cel - sis glo - ri - a.
in ex - cel - sis glo - - - - ri - a.
in ex - cel - sis glo - - ri - a.

17

f

When Christ was born of Ma - ry free, In Beth-lem in that fair ci - ty,

f

When Christ was born of Ma - ry free, In Beth-lem in that fair ci - ty,

f

When Christ was born of Ma - ry free, In Beth-lem in that fair ci - ty,

f

When Christ was born of Ma - ry free, In Beth-lem in that fair ci - ty,

22

mf

An - gels sung e'er with mirth and glee, in ex-cel-sis glo - ri - a.

mp

An - gels sung e'er with mirth and glee, glo - ri - a.

mp

An - gels sung e'er with mirth and glee, glo - ri - a.

mp

An - gels sung e'er with mirth and glee, glo - ri - a.

28
f
Chri-sto pa - re - mus can - - ti - ca,
f
Chri-sto pa-re - mus can - ti - ca,
f
Chri-sto pa-re - mus can - ti - ca, can - ti - ca,
f
Chri-sto pa-re - mus can - ti - ca, can - ti - ca,

32
in ex-cel - sis glo - - ri - a.
in ex-cel - sis glo - ri - a.
in ex-cel - sis glo - - - - ri - a.
in ex-cel - sis glo - - ri - a.

36

f

an-gels bright, To them ap-pear-èd with great light, And

f

an-gels bright, To them ap-pear-èd with great light, And

f

Herd-men be-held these an-gels bright, To them ap-pear-èd with great light, And

f

Herd-men be-held these an-gels bright, To them ap-pear-èd with great light, And

rit. - - - A little slower

40

mf

said, 'God's son is born this night.' This King is come to save his kind,

mp

said, *Ah* ________

mp

said, *Ah* ________

mp

said, *Ah* ________

rit. - - - A little slower

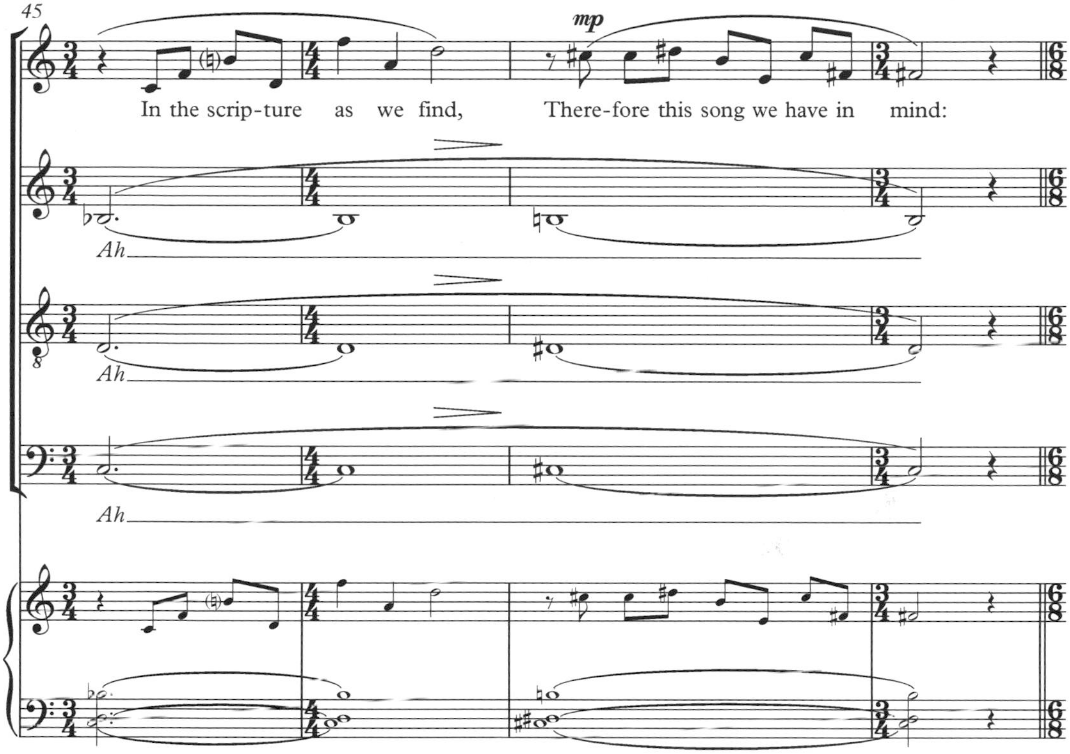
45
mp
In the scrip-ture as we find, There-fore this song we have in mind:
Ah
Ah
Ah

49
a tempo
mp
Chri-sto pa - re - mus can - - ti - ca,
mp
Chri-sto pa - re - mus can - ti - ca,
mp
Chri-sto pa - re - mus can - ti - ca, can - ti - ca,
mp
Chri-sto pa - re - mus can - ti - ca, can - ti - ca,
a tempo

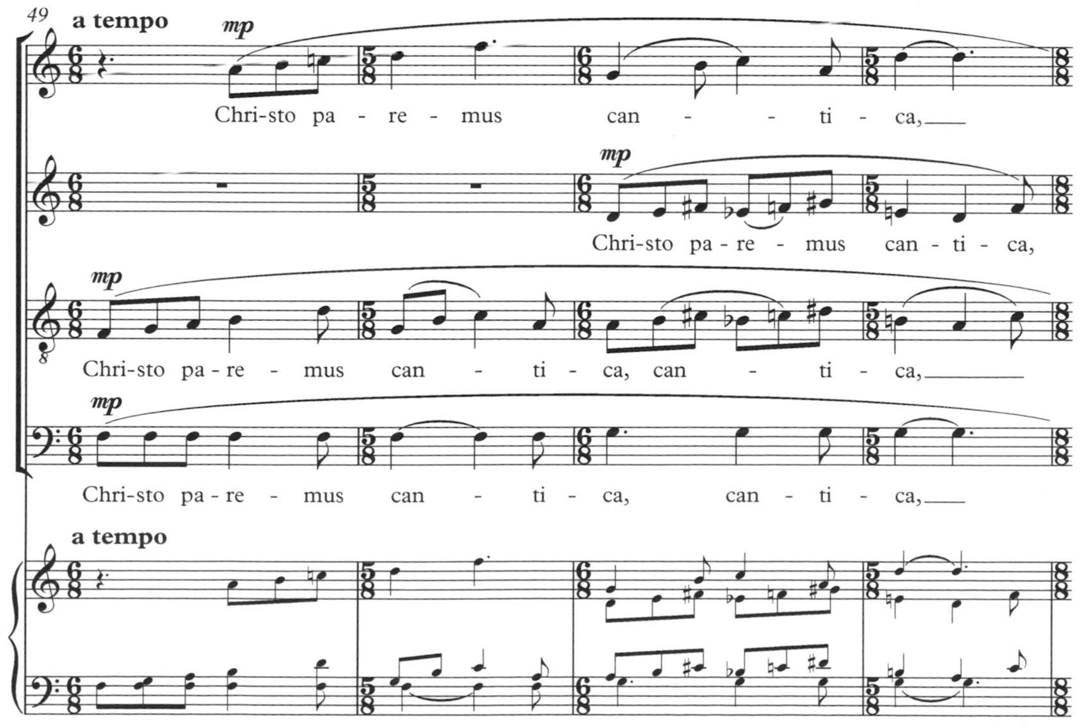

cresc.
53
in ex-cel - sis glo - - ri - a.
cresc.
in ex-cel - sis glo - ri - a.
cresc.
in ex-cel - sis glo - - - - ri - a.
cresc.
in ex-cel - sis glo - - ri - a.
A little slower
57
f
Then, dear Lord, for thy great grace, Grant us the bliss to
f
Then, dear Lord, for thy great grace, Grant us the bliss to
f
Then, dear Lord, for thy great grace, Grant us the bliss to
f
Then, dear Lord, for thy great grace, Grant us the bliss to
A little slower

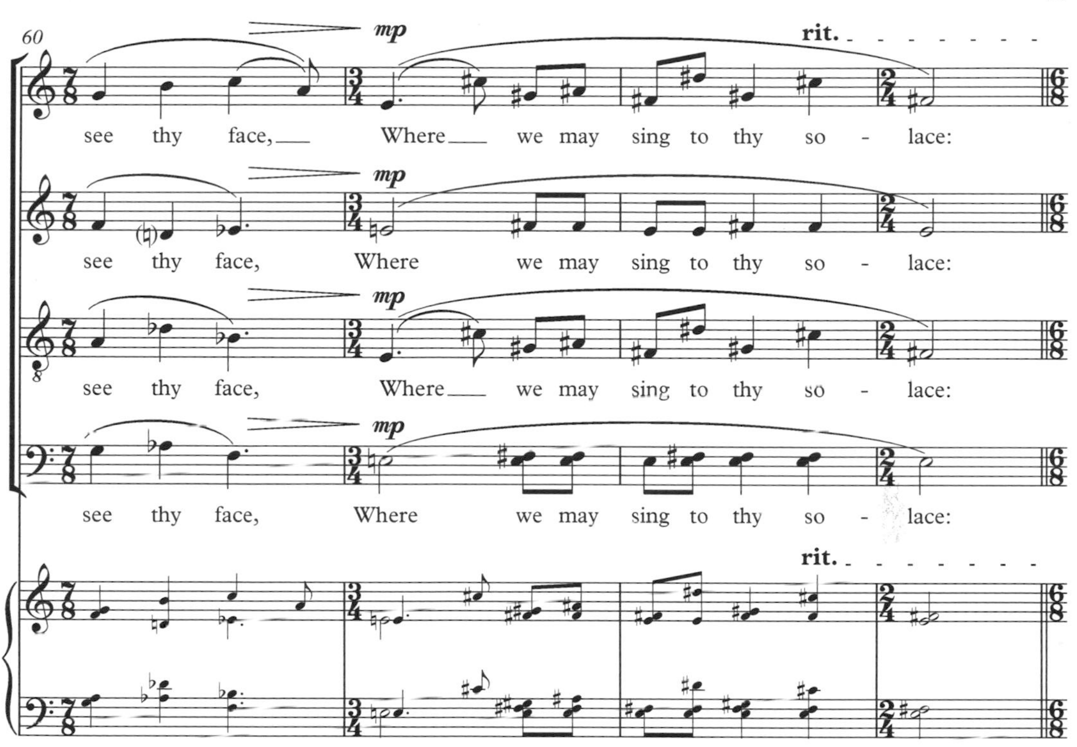

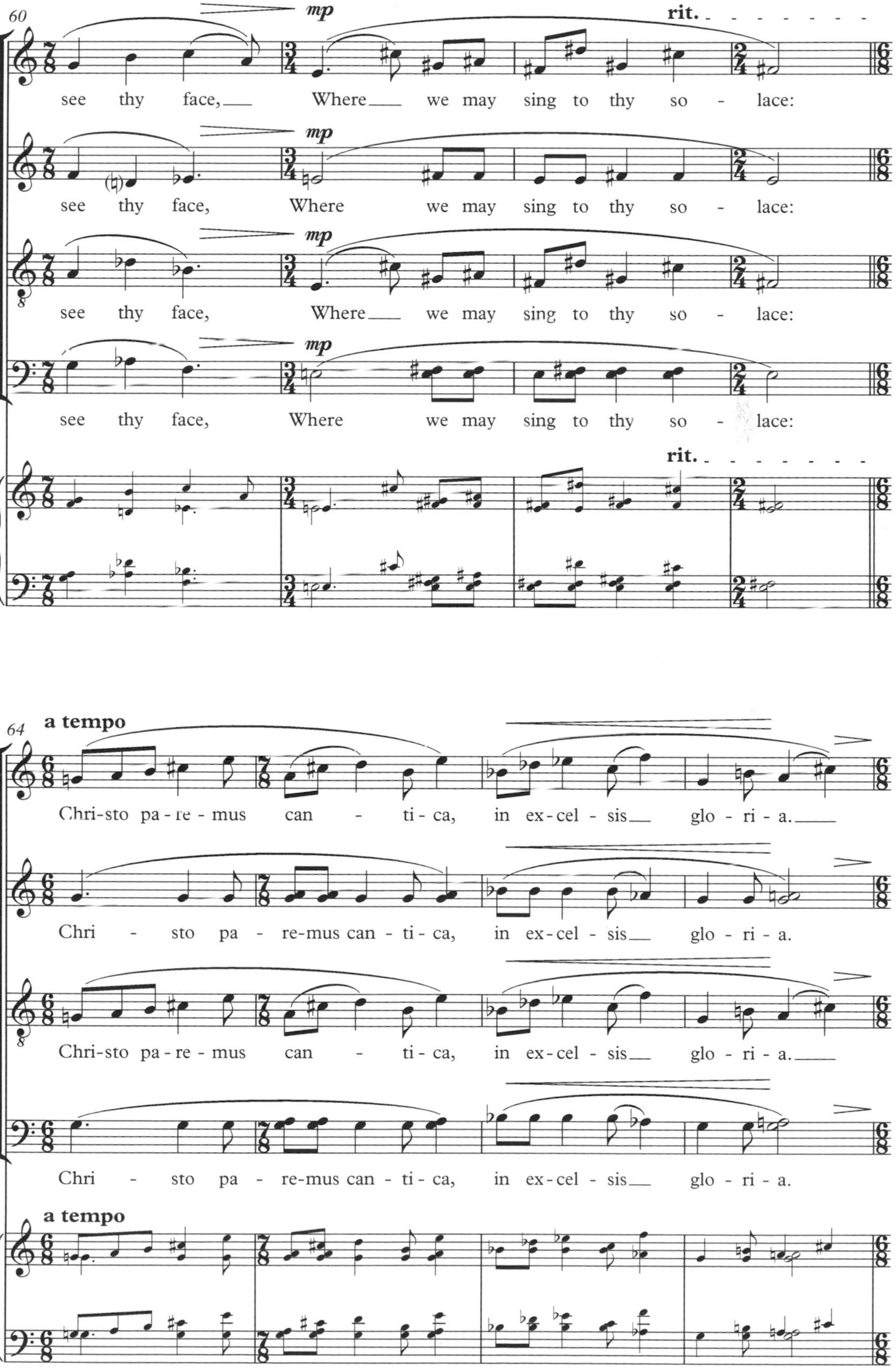
60
mp
rit.
see thy face, Where we may sing to thy so - lace:
see thy face, Where we may sing to thy so - lace:
see thy face, Where we may sing to thy so - lace:
see thy face, Where we may sing to thy so - lace:
rit.
64
a tempo
Chri-sto pa-re-mus can - ti-ca, in ex-cel-sis glo-ri-a.
Chri - sto pa - re-mus can - ti-ca, in ex-cel-sis glo-ri-a.
Chri-sto pa-re-mus can - ti-ca, in ex-cel-sis glo-ri-a.
Chri - sto pa - re-mus can - ti-ca, in ex-cel-sis glo-ri-a.
a tempo

68

mf

Chri-sto pa - re - mus can - - ti - ca,

mf

Chri-sto pa-re - mus can - ti - ca,

mf

Chri-sto pa-re - mus can - ti - ca, can - ti - ca,

mf

Chri-sto pa-re - mus can - ti - ca, can - ti - ca,

72

f

Chri-sto pa-re-mus can-ti-ca, in ex-cel-sis glo - ri-a,

f

Chri-sto pa-re-mus can-ti-ca, in ex-cel-sis glo - ri-a,

f

Chri-sto pa-re-mus can-ti-ca, in ex-cel-sis glo - ri-a,

f

Chri-sto pa-re-mus can-ti-ca, in ex-cel-sis glo - ri-a,

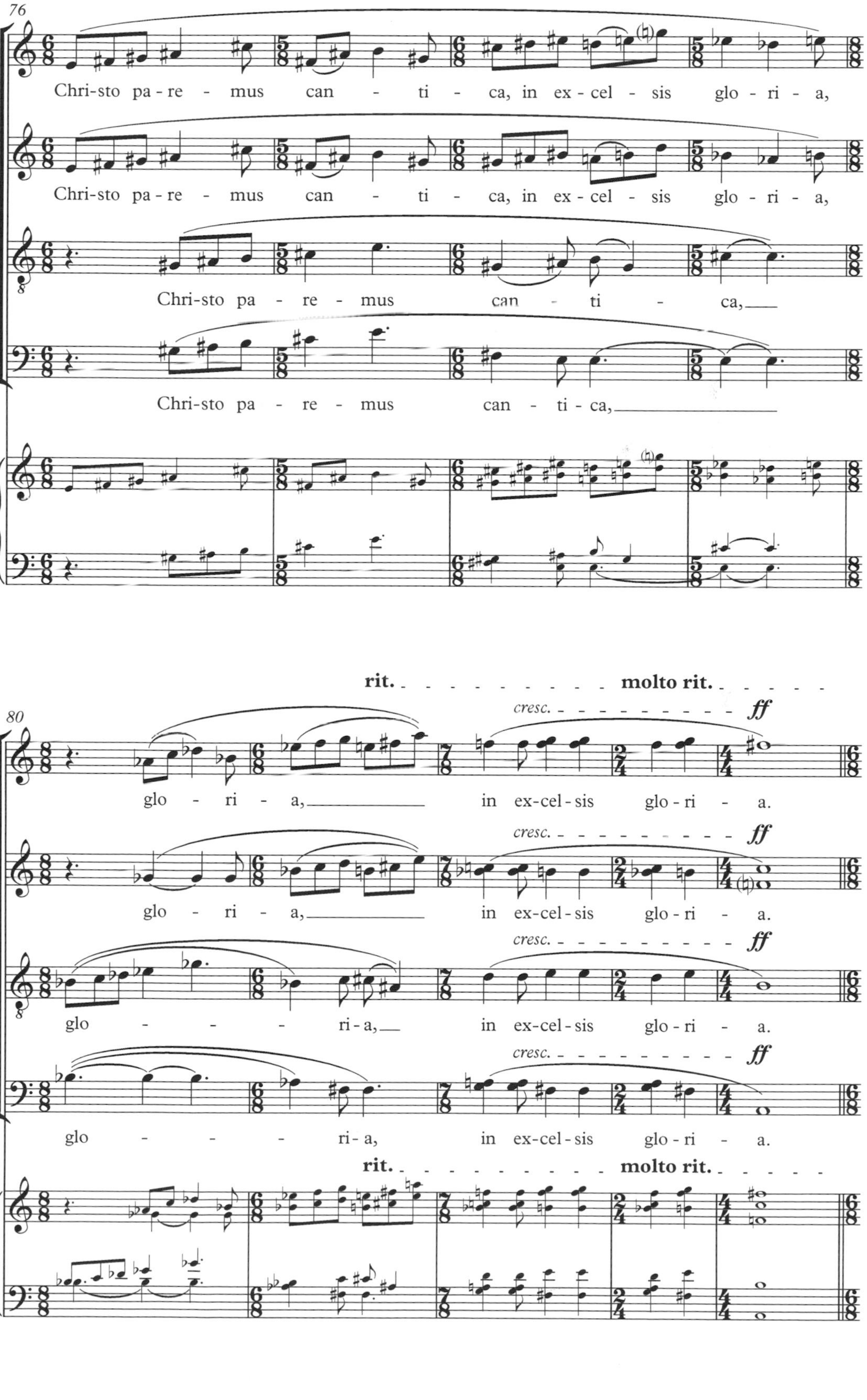

rit. . . . . molto rit. . . . . . .

80

cresc. . . . . ff

glo - ri - a, in ex-cel-sis glo - ri - a.

cresc. . . . . ff

glo - ri - a, in ex-cel-sis glo - ri - a.

cresc. . . . . ff

glo - - - ri - a, in ex-cel-sis glo - ri - a.

cresc. . . . . ff

glo - - - ri - a, in ex-cel-sis glo - ri - a.

rit. . . . . molto rit. . . . . . .

85

becoming faster - a tempo

mp

Chri-sto pa - re - mus can - ti - ca, in ex-cel - sis

mp

Chri-sto pa-re - mus can-ti - ca,

mp

Chri-sto pa-re - mus can - ti - ca, can - ti - ca, in ex-cel - sis

mp

Chri-sto pa-re - mus can - ti - ca, can - ti - ca, in ex-cel - sis

becoming faster - a tempo

A little slower

90

p

glo - - ri - a.

p

in ex-cel - sis glo - ri - a, glo - ri - a.

p

glo - - - - ri - a, glo - ri - a.

p

glo - - ri - a.

A little slower

God rest you merry, gentlemen

English traditional
arr. David Willcocks (b.1919)

* If preferred, the refrain may always be sung in unison (with organ accompaniment).

Unaccompanied voices

2. From God our heav'nly Father
A blessed angel came,
And unto certain shepherds
Brought tidings of the same,
How that in Bethlehem was born
The Son of God by name:
O tidings of comfort and joy.

Unison voices (with organ)

3. The shepherds at those tidings
Rejoicèd much in mind,
And left their flocks a-feeding,
In tempest, storm and wind,
And went to Bethlehem straightway
This blessèd babe to find:
O tidings of comfort and joy.

Unaccompanied voices

4. But when to Bethlehem they came,
Whereat this infant lay,
They found him in a manger,
Where oxen feed on hay;
His mother Mary kneeling,
Unto the Lord did pray:
O tidings of comfort and joy.

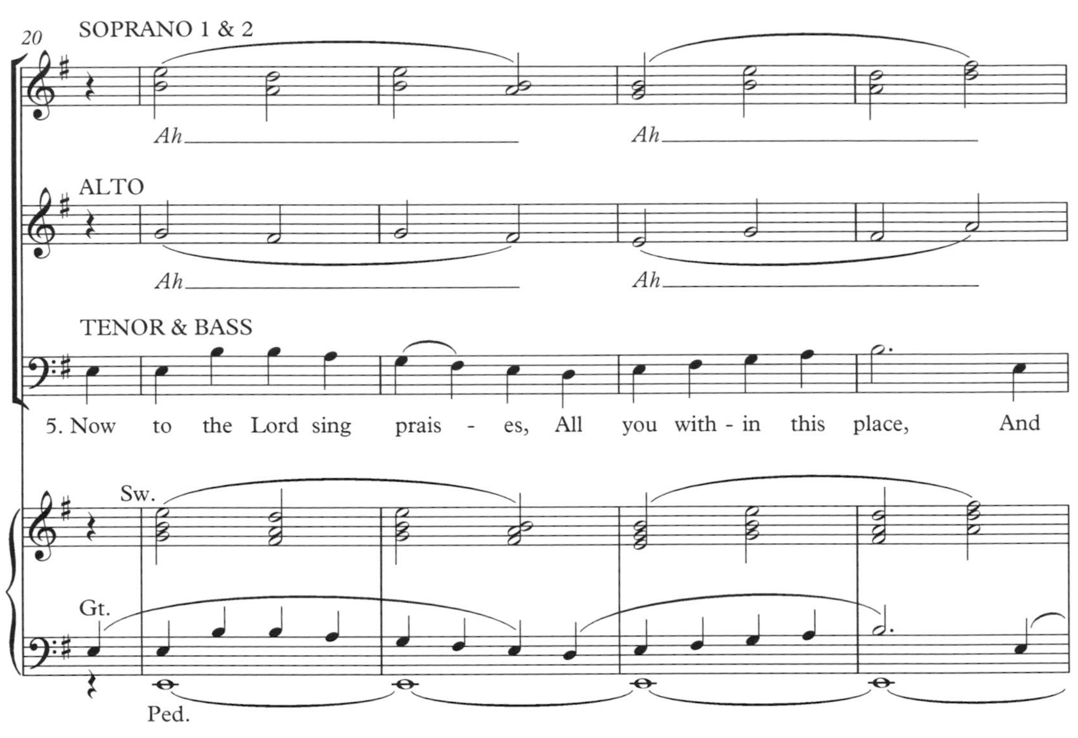
20
SOPRANO 1 & 2
Ah
Ah
ALTO
Ah
Ah
TENOR & BASS
5. Now to the Lord sing prais - es, All you with - in this place, And
Sw.
Gt.
Ped.

25
Ah
Ah
Ah
Ah
Ah
Ah
with true love and bro-ther-hood Each o - ther now em - brace; This ho - ly tide of

30
O tid - ings of com - fort and
O tid - ings of com - fort and
Christ - mas All o - thers doth de - face: O tid - ings of com - fort and
Gt.

35
joy, com-fort and joy, O tid - ings of com - fort and joy.
joy, com-fort and joy, O tid - ings of com - fort and joy.
joy, com-fort and joy, O tid - ings of com - fort and joy.

Good King Wenceslas

J.M. Neale
(1818–66)

14th century
arr. Stephen Cleobury

13
Bright - ly shone the moon that night, Though the frost was cru - el,
Bright - ly shone the moon that night, Though the frost was cru - el,
Bright - ly shone the moon that night, Though the frost was cru - el,
Bright - ly shonc the moon that night, Though the frost was cru - el,
17
mp
When a poor man came in sight, Gath-'ring win-ter fu - - el.
When a poor man came in sight, Gath-'ring win-ter fu - - el.
When a poor man came in sight, Gath-'ring win-ter fu - - el.
When a poor man came in sight, Gath-'ring win-ter fu - - el.
22
TENOR 1
mf
2.'Hi - ther, page, and stand by me, If thou know'st it, tell - ing,
TENOR 2
mf
2.'Hi - ther, page, and stand by me, If thou know'st it, tell - ing,
BASS
f
2.'Hi - ther, page, and stand by me, If thou know'st it, tell - ing,
16'
mf

26
ALTO 1
mf
Yon - der pea - sant, who is he? Where and what his dwell - ing?'
ALTO 2
mf
Yon - der, who is he? Where and what his dwell - ing?'
(f)
Yon - der pea - sant, who is he? Where and what his dwell - ing?'
30
S.
mf
'Sire, he lives a good league hence, Un - der - neath the moun - tain,
A.
T.
mf
'Sire, he lives a good league hence, Un - der-neath the
B.
mf
'Sire, he lives a good league
34
Right a-gainst the fo - rest fence, By Saint Ag - nes' foun - tain.'
mf
Right a - gainst the fo - rest fence, By Saint Ag - nes' foun - tain.
moun- tain. Right a - gainst the fo - rest fence, By Saint Ag - nes' foun - tain.
hence, By Saint Ag - nes' foun - tain.'

39
ALTO 1 mf
Thou
TENOR 1
mf
3. 'Bring me flesh and bring me wine, Bring me pine logs hi - ther,
TENOR 2
mf
3. 'Bring me flesh and bring me wine, Bring me pine logs hi - ther,
BASS
f
3. 'Bring me flesh and bring me wine, Bring me pine logs hi - ther,
Ped.
mf
43
ALTO 1
and I will see him dine, When we bear them thi - ther.'
ALTO 2
mf
Thou and I will see him dine, When we bear them thi - ther.'
TENOR
Thou and I will see him dine, When we bear them thi - ther.'
BASS
Thou and I will see him dine, When we bear them thi - ther.'
47
SOPRANO
f
Page and mo-narch, forth they went, Forth they went to - ge - ther
A. f
Page and mo-narch, forth they went, Forth they went to - ge - ther
T. f
Page and mo - narch, forth they went, Forth they went to - ge - ther
B. f
Page and mo-narch, forth they went, Forth they went to - ge - ther

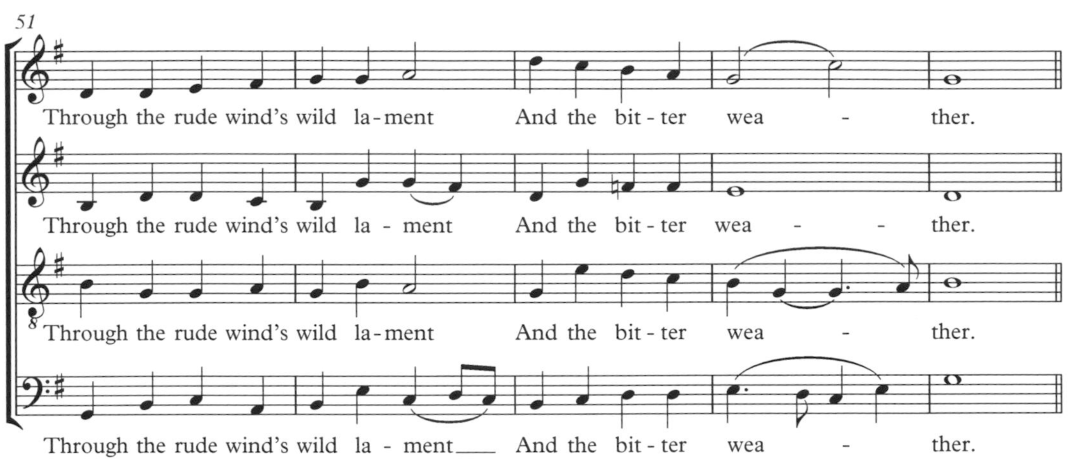
51
Through the rude wind's wild la-ment And the bit-ter wea - ther.
Through the rude wind's wild la - ment And the bit-ter wea - - ther.
Through the rude wind's wild la-ment And the bit-ter wea - ther.
Through the rude wind's wild la - ment And the bit-ter wea - ther.

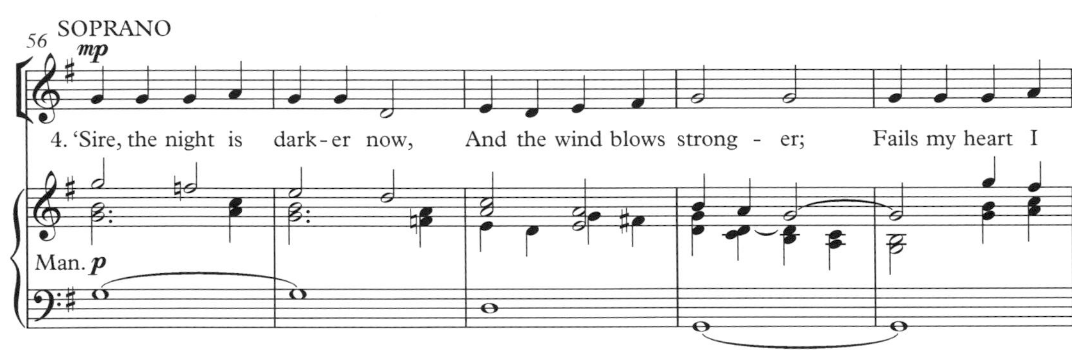
56 SOPRANO
mp
4. 'Sire, the night is dark-er now, And the wind blows strong - er; Fails my heart I
Man. p

61 (S.)
know not how; I can go no long - er.'
TENOR mf
'Mark my foot-steps, good my page;
BASS mf
'Mark my foot-steps, good my page;
mf
mf

66
(S.)
(A.)
T.
Tread thou in them bold - ly: Thou shalt find the win-ter's rage Freeze thy blood less
B.
Tread thou in them bold - ly: Thou shalt find the win-ter's rage Freeze thy blood less
71
f
5. In his mas-ter's steps he trod,
5. In his mas-ter's steps he trod, Where
cold - ly.'
5. In his mas-ter's steps he trod, Where
cold - ly.'
5. In his mas-ter's steps he trod,
cresc.

76
Where snow lay dinted; Heat was in the very sod
the snow lay dinted; Heat was in the very sod
the snow lay dinted; Heat was in the very sod
Where the snow lay dinted; Heat was in the very sod
80
SOPRANO 1
which the saint had printed.
SOPRANO 2
which the saint had printed. There-fore Christ-ian
Which the saint had printed. There-fore Christ-ian men be
Which the saint had printed. There-fore Christ-ian men be
Which the saint had printed. There-fore Christ-ian men be sure,

84
Wealth or rank pos - sess - ing, Ye who bless the poor, Shall your -
men Wealth pos - sess - ing, Ye who bless the poor, Shall your -
sure, Wealth pos - sess - ing, Ye who now will bless the poor,
sure, Wealth pos - sess - ing, Ye who now will bless the poor,
Wealth or rank pos - sess - ing, Ye who now will bless the poor,
88
-selves find bless - - - - - - - ing.
shall your-selves find bless - - - ing.
shall your-selves find bless - - - ing.
shall your-selves find bless - - - ing.

I saw three ships come sailing in

English traditional
arr. Simon Preston (b.1938)

13
what was in those ships all three? On Christ-mas Day in the morn - ing.
17
SOLO
3. Our
21
Sa - viour Christ and his la - dy, On Christ-mas Day, on Christ-mas Day, Our
mp
Ped.
25
Sa - viour Christ and his la - dy, On Christ-mas Day in the morn - ing.
dim.

29
S.
TUTTI mf
On Christ-mas Day, on
ALTO mf
On Christ-mas Day, on
TENOR SOLO f
dim.
4. Pray, whi - ther sailed those ships all three?
(BASS)
33
Christ - mas Day,
Christ - mas Day,
f
dim.
Pray, whi - ther sailed those ships all three?
37
mf
rall.
On Christ-mas Day, on Christ-mas Day, On Christ - mas Day in the morn -
mf
On Christ-mas Day, on Christ-mas Day, On Christ - mas Day in the morn -
TUTTI mf
On Christ - mas Day in the morn -
BASS mf
On Christ - mas Day in the morn -

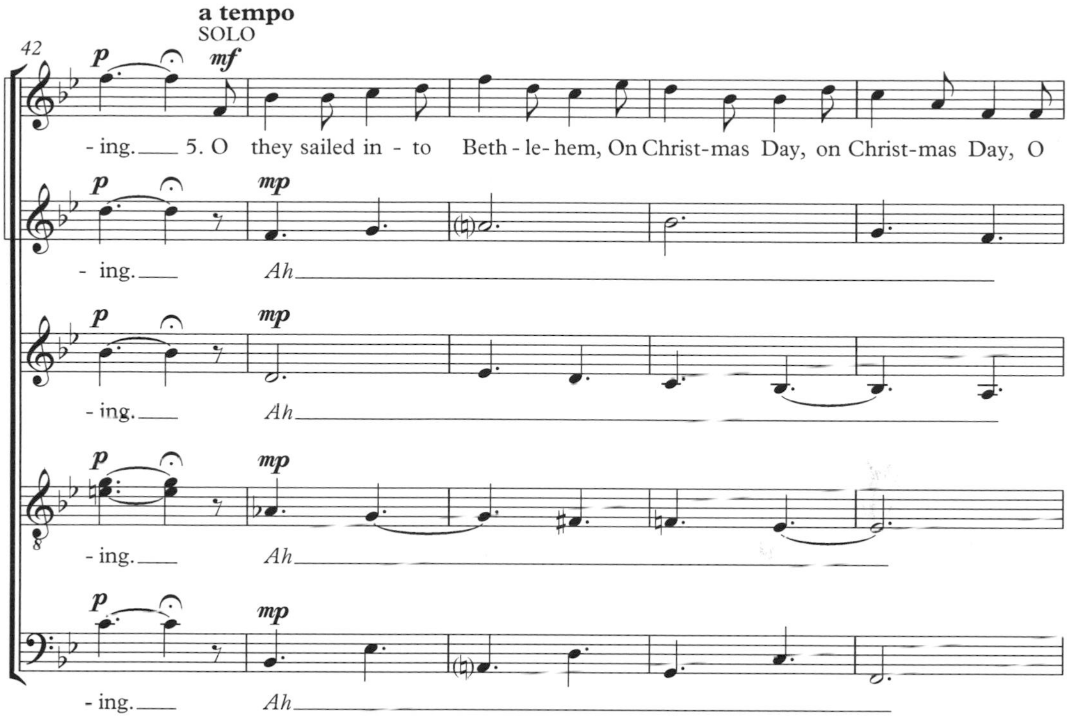

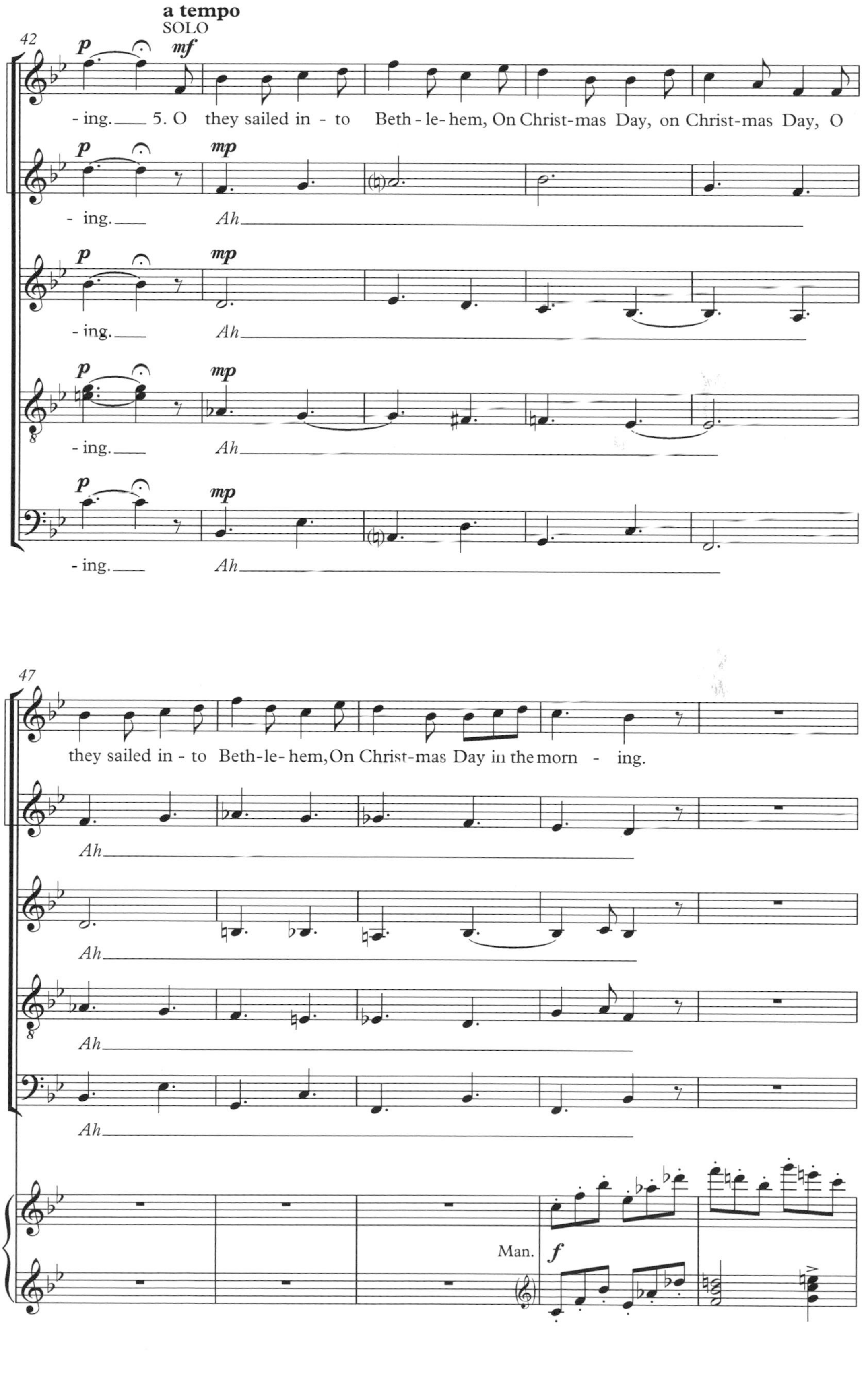
a tempo
SOLO
42
p
mf
- ing. 5. O they sailed in - to Beth - le - hem, On Christ-mas Day, on Christ-mas Day, O
mp
- ing. Ah
- ing. Ah
- ing. Ah
- ing. Ah
47
they sailed in - to Beth - le - hem, On Christ-mas Day in the morn - ing.
Ah
Ah
Ah
Ah
Man.
f

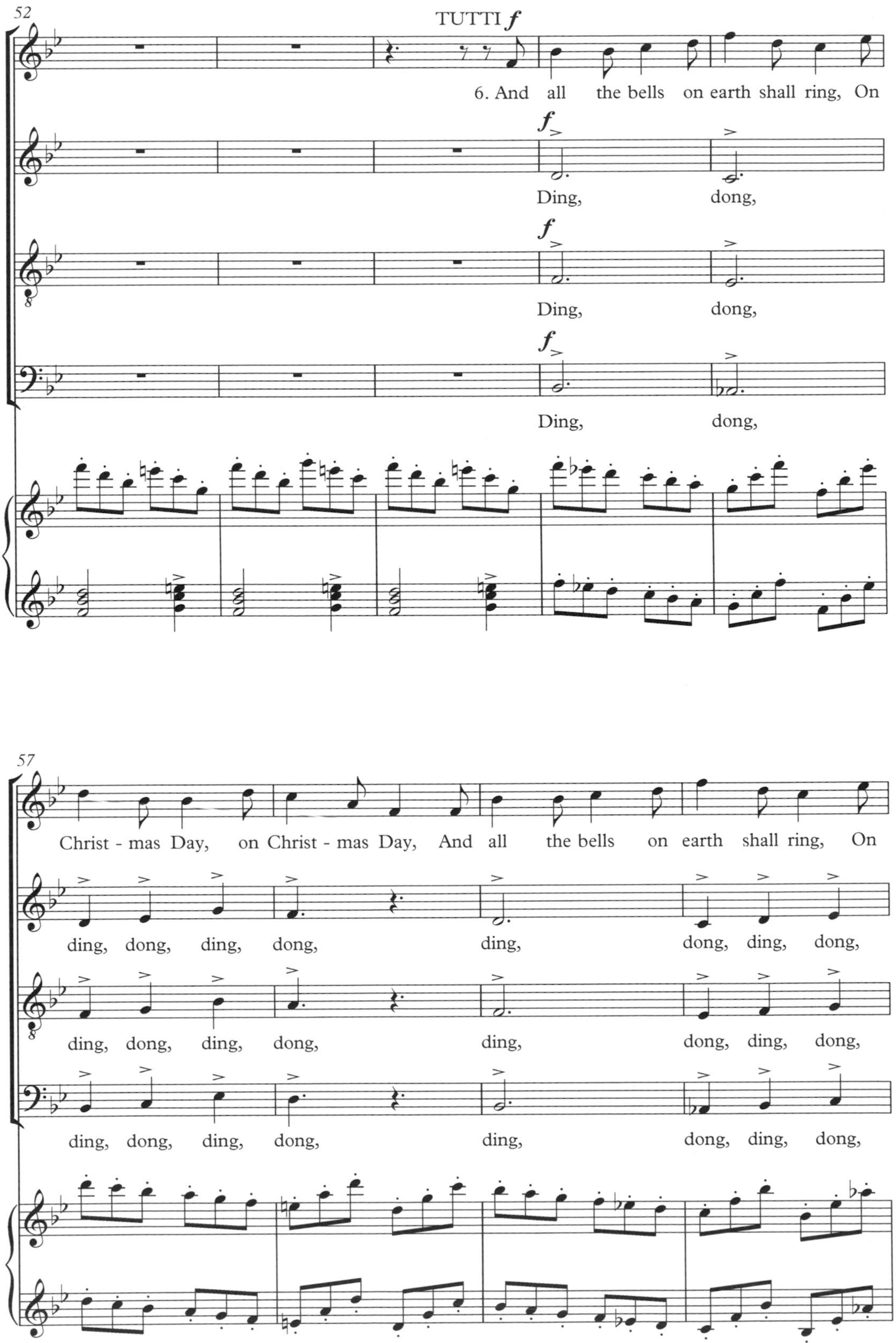

52

TUTTI *f*

6. And all the bells on earth shall ring, On

f
Ding, dong,

f
Ding, dong,

f
Ding, dong,

61
Christ-mas Day in the morn - ing.
ding, dong.
ding, dong.
ding, dong.
(solo stop)
66
un poco sostenuto
mf espress.
cresc.
7. And all the an-gels in heav'n shall sing, On Christ-mas Day, on Christ-mas Day, And
7. And all the an-gels in heav'n shall sing, On Christ-mas Day, on Christ-mas Day, And
7. And all the an-gels in heav'n shall sing, On Christ-mas Day, on Christ-mas Day, And
7. And all the an-gels in heav'n shall sing, On Christ-mas Day, on Christ-mas Day, And
un poco sostenuto
71
ten.
a tempo
p
f
all the an-gels in heav'n shall sing, On Christ-mas Day in the morn - ing.
all the an-gels in heav'n shall sing, in the morn - ing.
all the an-gels in heav'n shall sing, in the morn - ing. 8. And
all the an-gels in heav'n shall sing, in the morn - ing. 8. And

75
T.
all the souls on earth shall sing, On Christ-mas Day, on Christ-mas Day, And all the souls on
B.
all the souls on earth shall sing, On Christ-mas Day, on Christ-mas Day, And all the souls on
f
Ped.
80
earth shall sing, On Christ-mas Day in the morn- ing.
earth shall sing, On Christ-mas Day in the morn- ing.
Man.
85
S.
Vivacissimo
f
9. Then let us all re - joice a- main! On
A.
9. Then let us all re - joice a - main! On
T.
9. Then let us all re - joice a - main! On
B.
9. Then let us all re - joice a - main! On
Vivacissimo

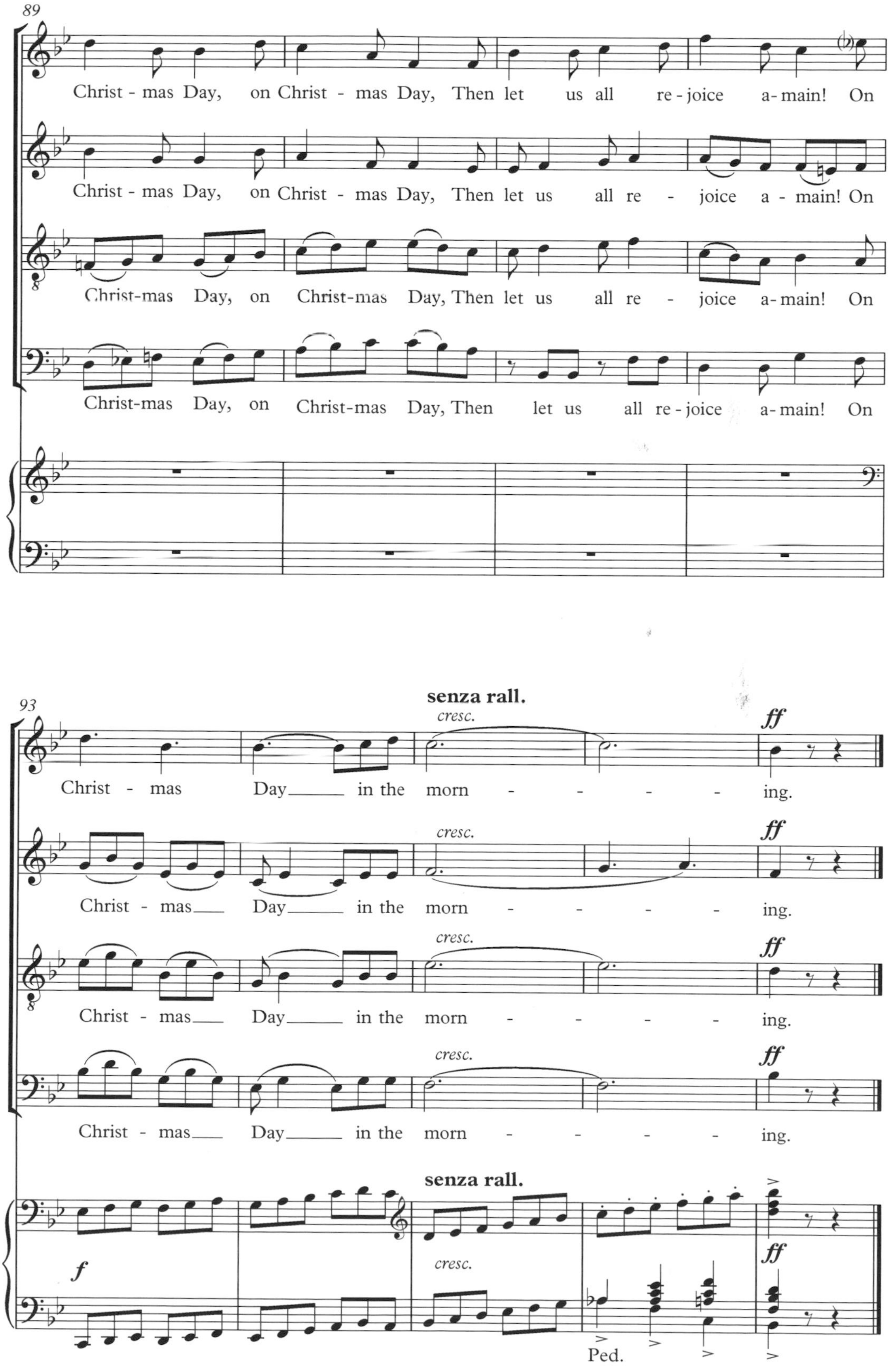

93

senza rall.

cresc. *ff*

Christ - mas Day___ in the morn - - - - - ing.

cresc. *ff*

Christ - mas___ Day___ in the morn - - - - - ing.

cresc. *ff*

Christ - mas___ Day___ in the morn - - - - - ing.

cresc. *ff*

Christ - mas___ Day___ in the morn - - - - - ing.

senza rall.

f *cresc.* *ff*

Ped.

to Stephen Jackson and the Wooburn Singers

I wonder as I wander

John Jacob Niles

Carl Rütti (b.1949)
Organ reduction by
Anne Duarte & Carl Rütti

Words and original music by John Jacob Niles

17
ff
f
poor on - 'ry peo - ple like you and like I. I won - der as I
ff
f
pp
cresc.
ff
mf
22
wan - der out un - der the sky.
p
28
p
f
When Ma - ry birthed Je - sus, 'twas in a cow's stall, with
p
f

33
pp
wise men and far-mers and shep-herds and all. But high from the
pp
f
pp
38
ff
f
hea-vens a star's light did fall, and pro-mise of ages it
ff
f
ff
mf
43
f
then did re-call. If
f
mf

49
Je - sus had wan - ted for a - ny wee thing,
a star in the
a star in the
ff
f
54
sky, or a bird on the wing,
sky, or a bird on the wing,
or all of God's an - gels in
pp
59
hea - ven for to sing, he sure - ly could have it, 'cause he was the King.
ff
f
p
mf
pp
poco rit.

to my mother

I sing of a maiden

Sloane MS. 2593 (15th century)

Patrick Hadley (1899–1973)

13
mp
grass. He came all so still To his mo - ther's
mp
grass. He came all so still To his mo - ther's
mp
Ped. Ped. Ped. Ped.
17
mf
mp
p
bower, As dew in A - pril that fall-eth on the flower. He
mf
mp
p
bower, As dew in A - pril that fall-eth on the flower. He
mf
mp
22
pp
came all so still Where his mo - ther lay, As
pp
came all so still Where his mo - ther lay, As
Ped. Ped. Ped. Ped.

26
Meno mosso
a tempo
dew in A - pril That fall - eth on the spray.
dew in A - pril That fall - eth on the spray.
Meno mosso
a tempo
pp
Ped.
Ped.
31
f
Mo-ther and mai-den Was ne-ver none but she:
pp
poco
Well may such a
Mo - ther and mai - den was ne-ver none but she:
Well may such a
f
pp
Ped.
34
ppp
la - dy God's mo - ther be.
la - dy God's mo - ther be.
p
ppp
Ped.
Ped.

Written for the Choir of King's College, Cambridge,
Festival of Nine Lessons and Carols, Christmas Eve 1985

Illuminare, Jerusalem

15th century
Bannatyne MS *f.*27v

Judith Weir
(b.1954)

[1] = star [2] = king

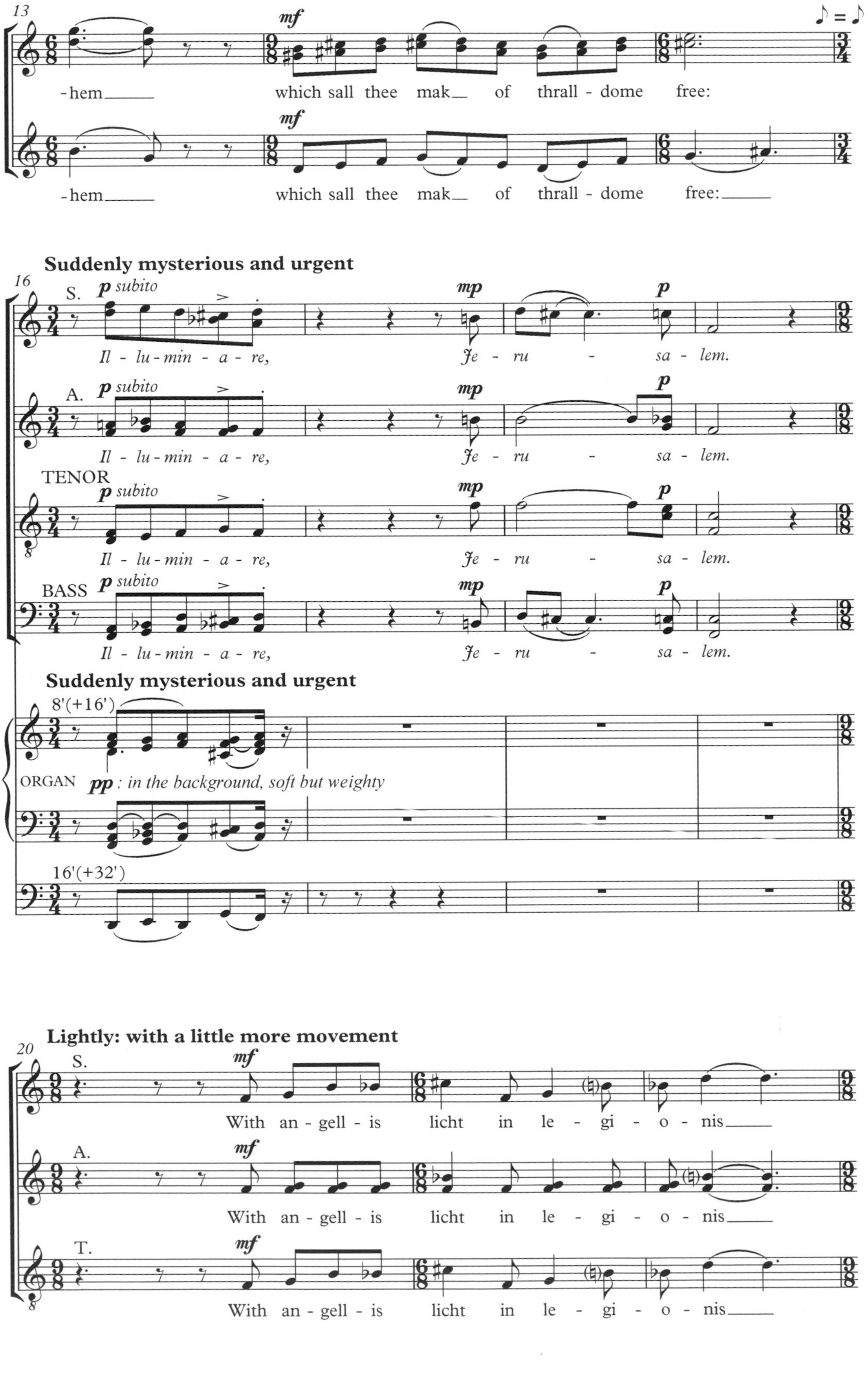

16

Suddenly mysterious and urgent

S. *p subito* *mp* *p*

Il - lu - min - a - re, Je - ru - sa - lem.

A. *p subito* *mp* *p*

Il - lu - min - a - re, Je - ru - sa - lem.

TENOR *p subito* *mp* *p*

Il - lu - min - a - re, Je - ru - sa - lem.

BASS *p subito* *mp* *p*

Il - lu - min - a - re, Je - ru - sa - lem.

Suddenly mysterious and urgent

8'(+16')

ORGAN **pp** : *in the background, soft but weighty*

16'(+32')

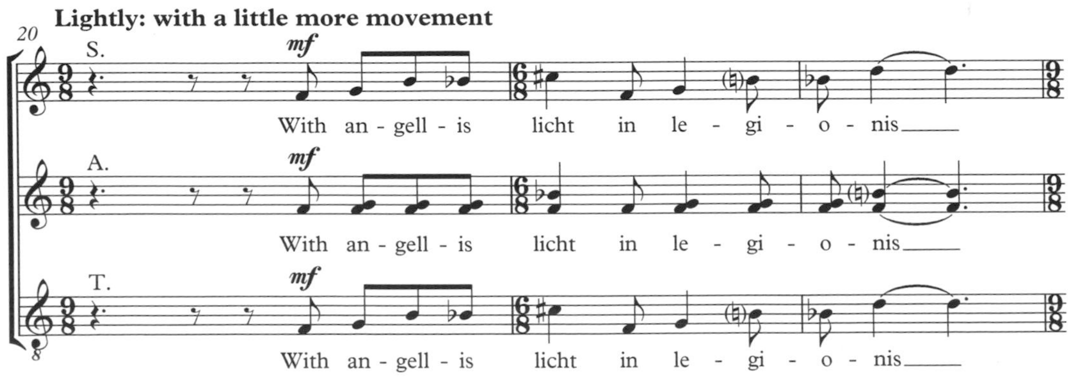

[1] = at once, all together

Mysterious and urgent
35
shou - t: Il - lu-min - a - re, Je - ru - sa-
BASS
Mysterious and urgent
39
a tempo: strong and deliberate (but not too slow)
- lem.
T.1
The rege-and tir-rant that in thee rang, He-rod, is ex-ile-it
T.2
The rege-and tir-rant that in thee rang, He - rod,
He - rod,

[1] = held, harboured [2] = worthy

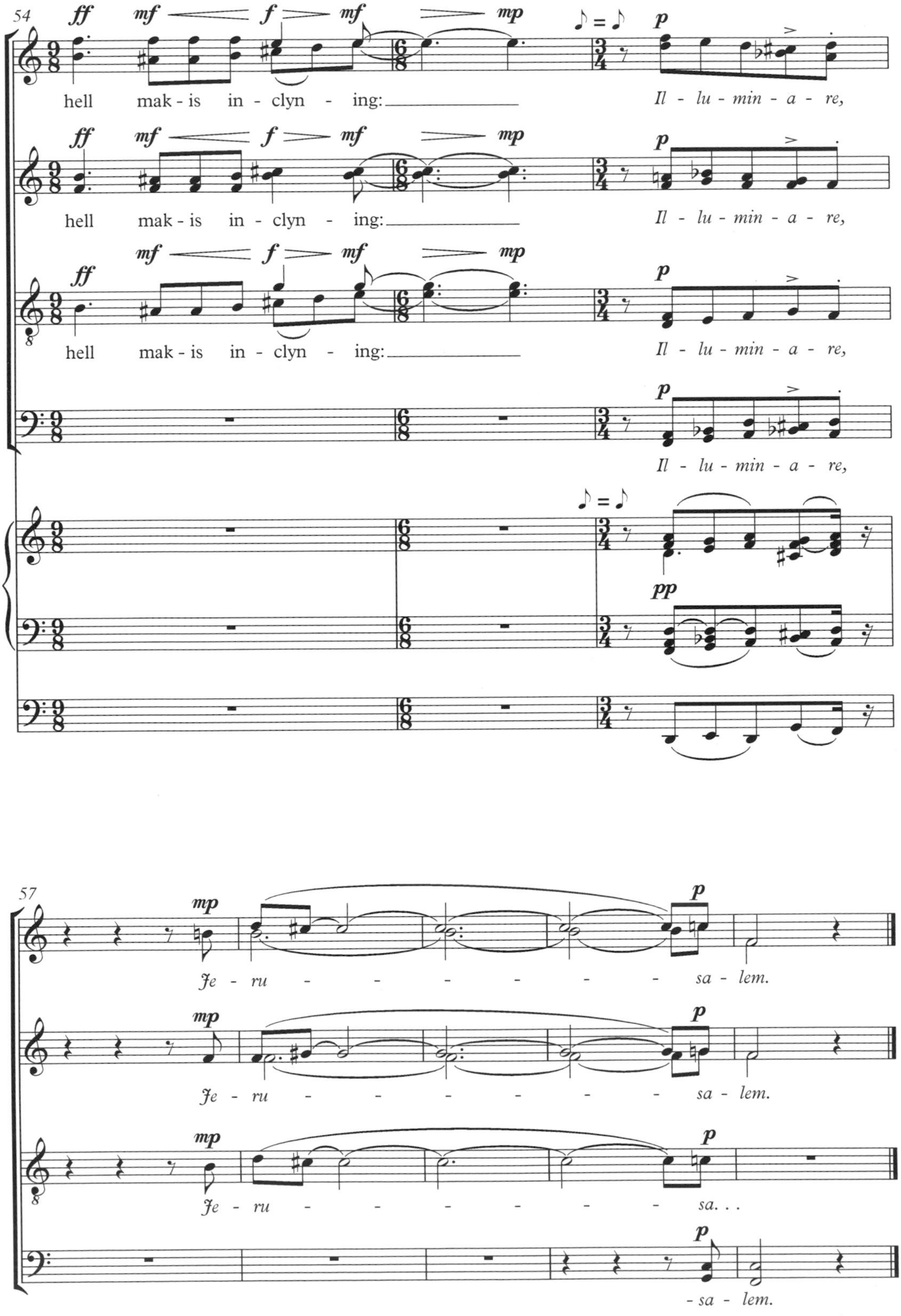

54

ff mf f mf mp ♪ = ♪ p

hell mak - is in - clyn - ing: *Il - lu - min - a - re,*

hell mak - is in - clyn - ing: *Il - lu - min - a - re,*

hell mak - is in - clyn - ing: *Il - lu - min - a - re,*

Il - lu - min - a - re,

pp

Commissioned by Stephen Cleobury and the Choir of King's College, Cambridge
for the Festival of Nine Lessons and Carols, Christmas Eve 1983

to Keith Miller-Jones

In wintertime

Betty Askwith (1909–95)

Lennox Berkeley (1903–89)

14
p
mp
- ship, wor - ship Thee. 2. The Three Wise
- ship, wor - ship, wor - ship Thee. 2. The Three Wise
- ship, wor - ship Thee. 2. The Three Wise
ship, wor - ship Thee. 2. The Three Wise

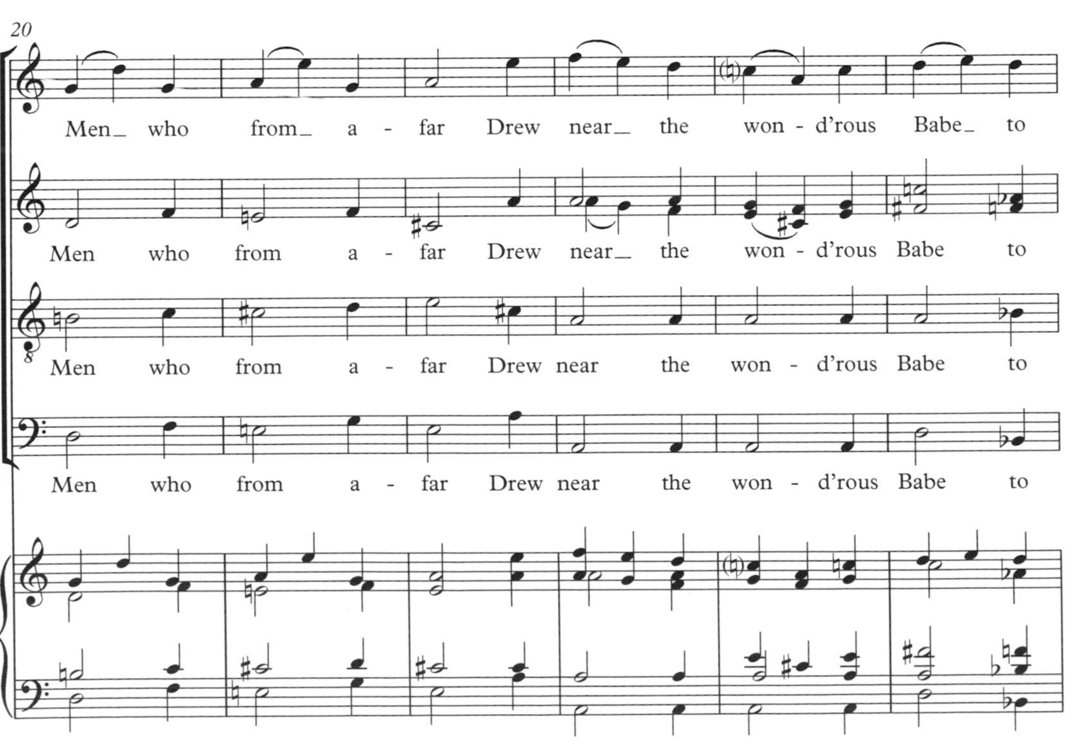
20
Men who from a - far Drew near the won - d'rous Babe to
Men who from a - far Drew near the won - d'rous Babe to
Men who from a - far Drew near the won - d'rous Babe to
Men who from a - far Drew near the won - d'rous Babe to

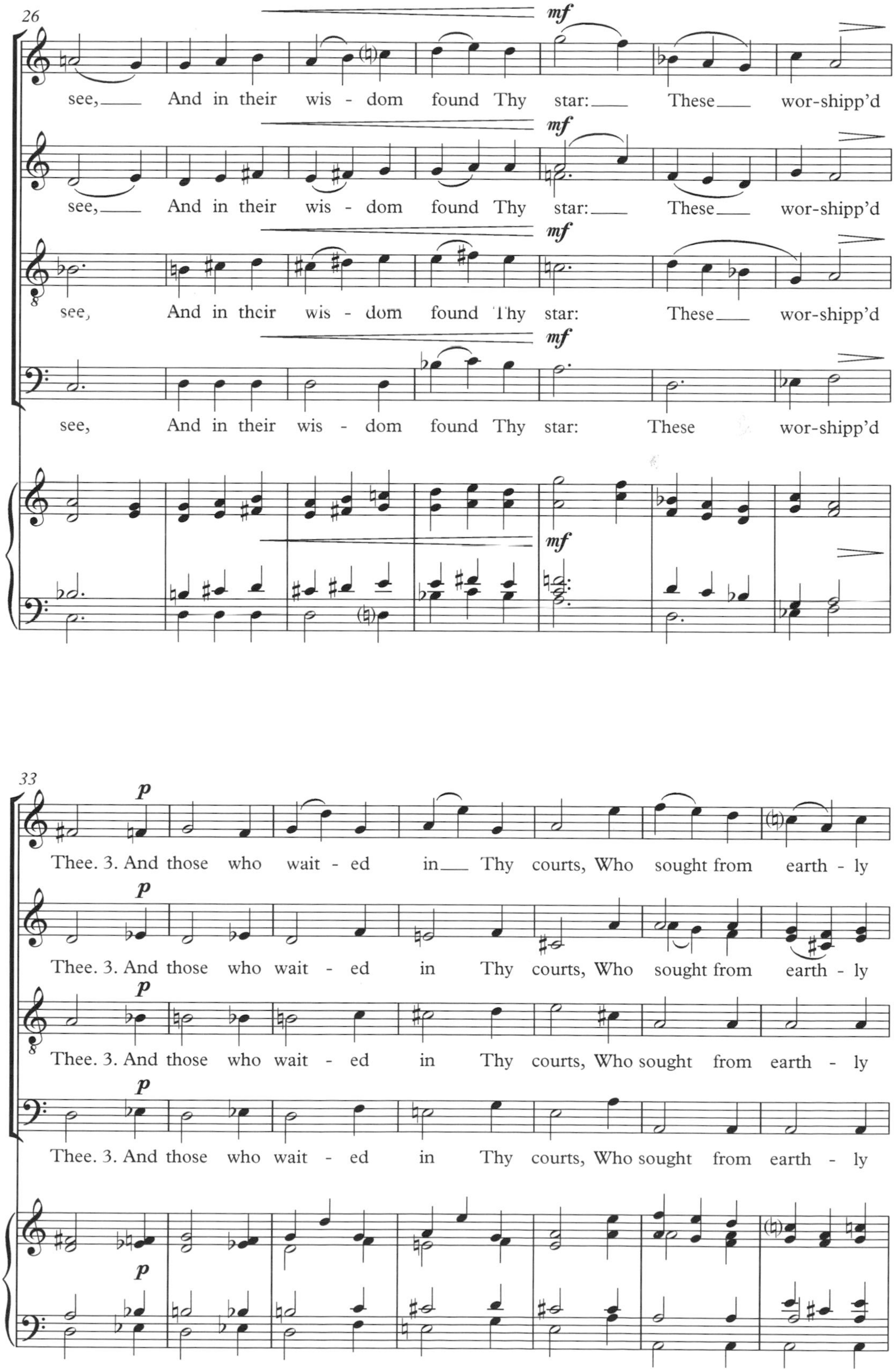

26

mf

see, And in their wis - dom found Thy star: These worship'd

see, And in their wis - dom found Thy star: These worship'd

see, And in their wis - dom found Thy star: These worship'd

see, And in their wis - dom found Thy star: These worship'd

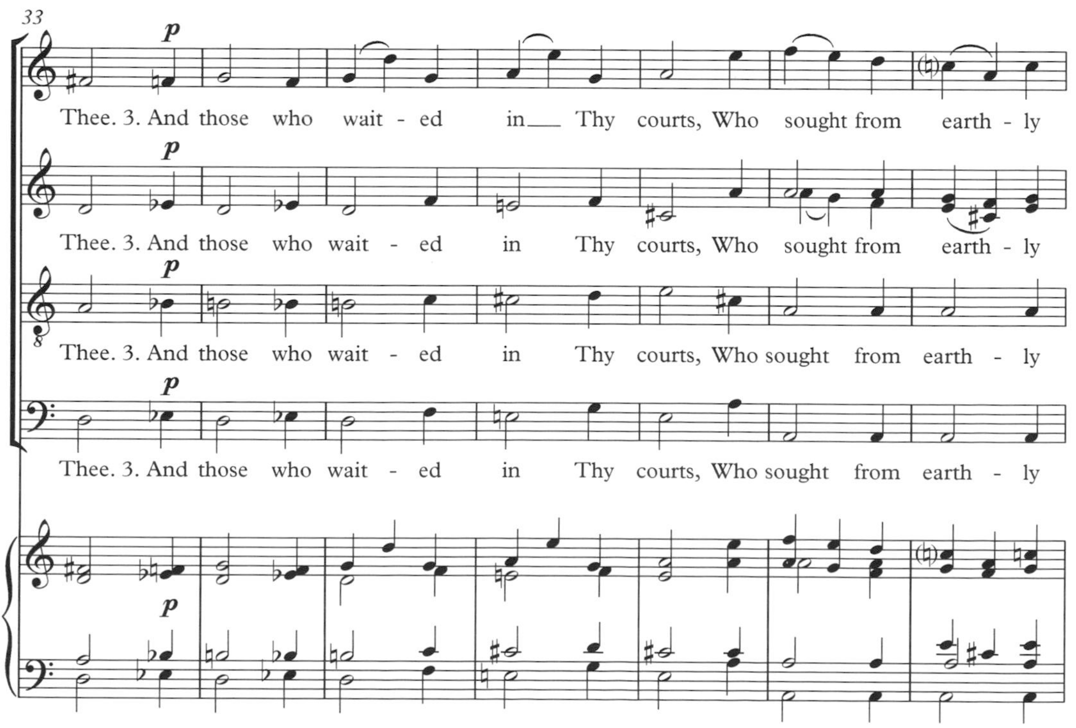

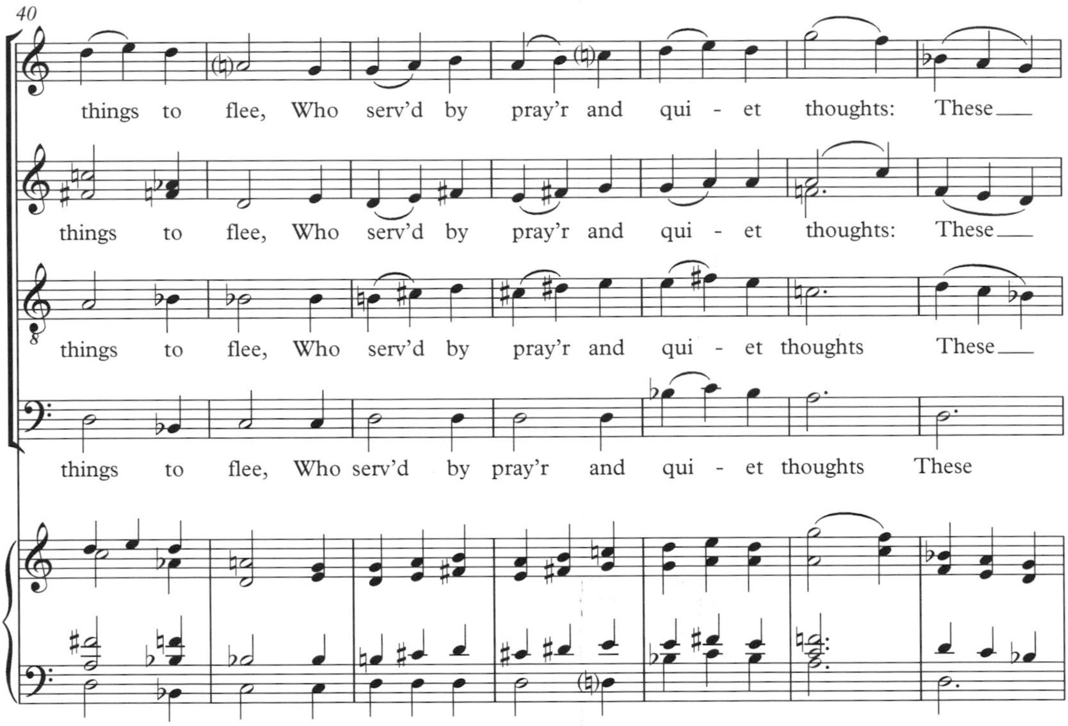
40
things to flee, Who serv'd by pray'r and qui - et thoughts: These
things to flee, Who serv'd by pray'r and qui - et thoughts: These
things to flee, Who serv'd by pray'r and qui - et thoughts These
things to flee, Who serv'd by pray'r and qui - et thoughts These

47
mp
wor-shipp'd Thee. 4. And shep-herds who sat watch-ing then, Their flocks a -
wor-shipp'd Thee. 4. And shep-herds who sat watch-ing then, Their flocks a -
wor-shipp'd Thee. 4. And shep-herds who sat watch-ing then, Their flocks a -
wor-shipp'd Thee. 4. And shep-herds who sat watch-ing then, Their flocks a -

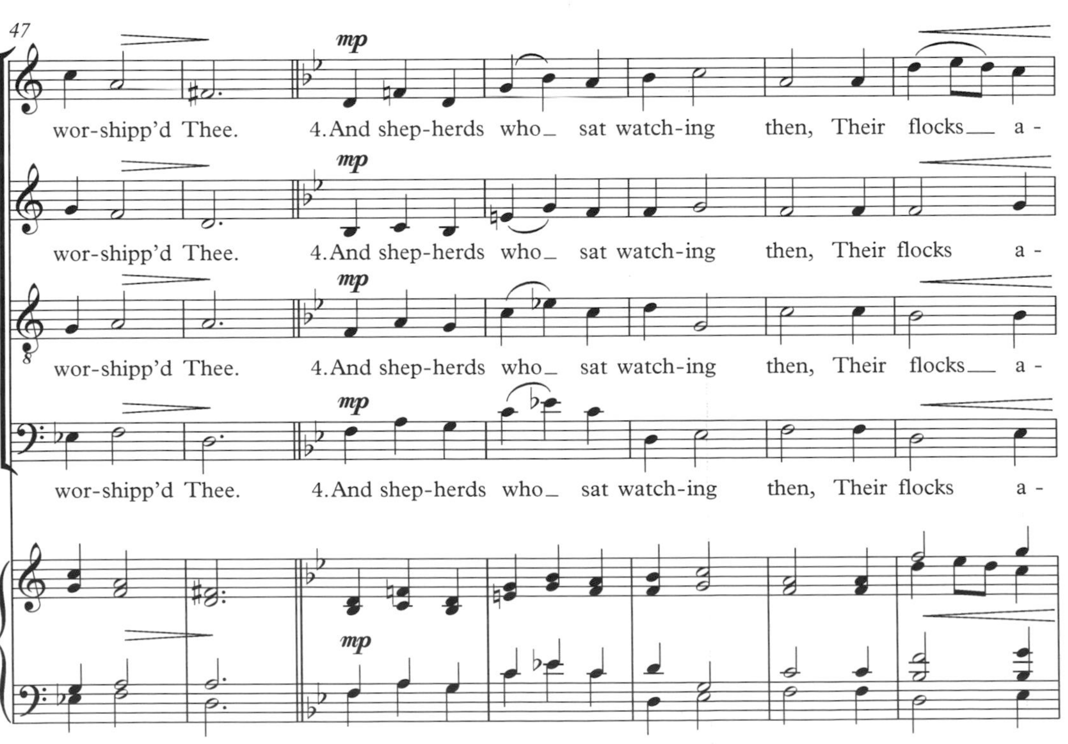

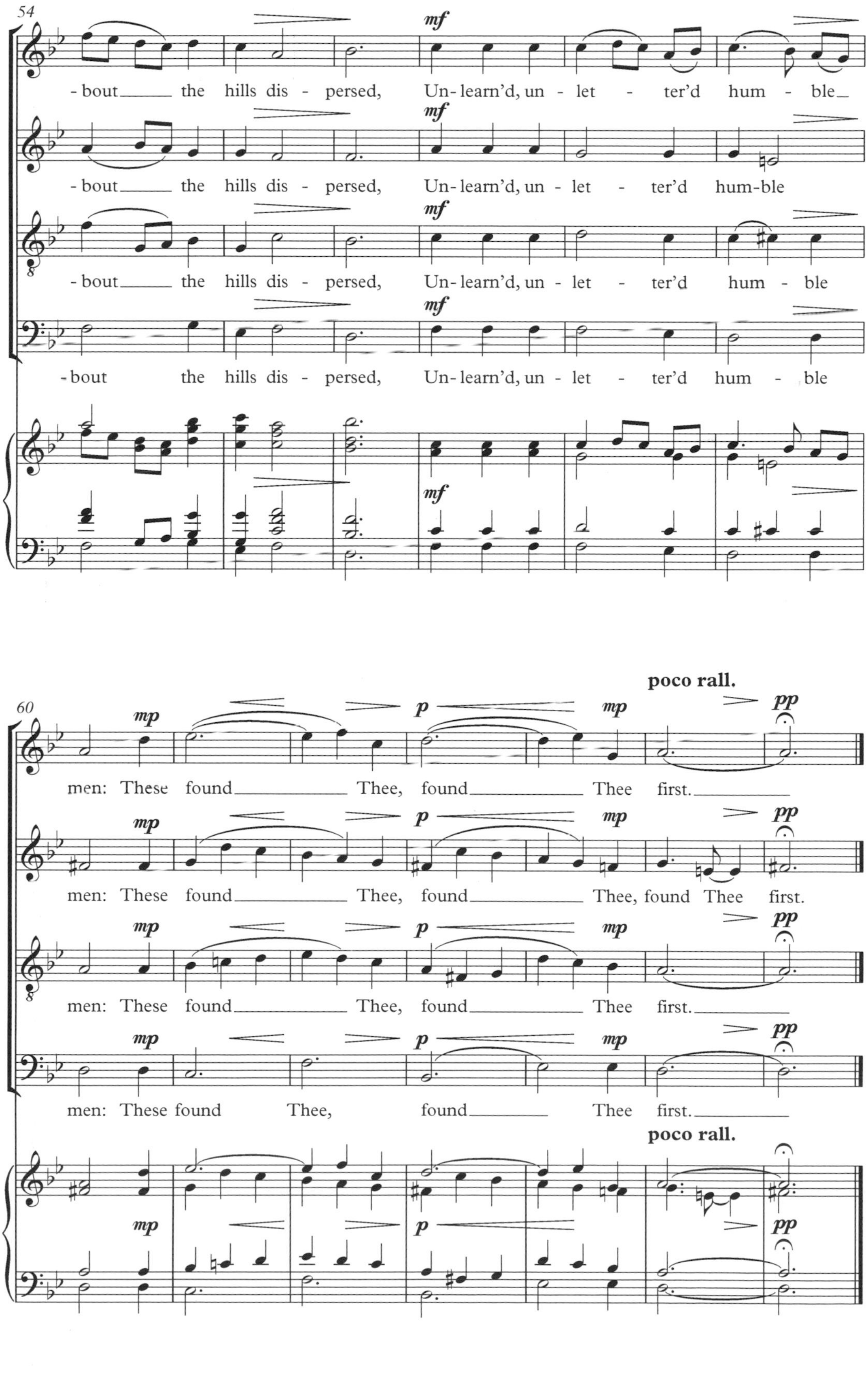

60
poco rall.
mp p mp pp
men: These found Thee, found Thee first.
mp p mp pp
men: These found Thee, found Thee, found Thee first.
mp p mp pp
men: These found Thee, found Thee first.
mp p mp pp
men: These found Thee, found Thee first.
poco rall.
mp p pp

Infant holy, infant lowly

(*W żłobie leży*)

tr. Edith M. Reed

Polish traditional
arr. Stephen Cleobury

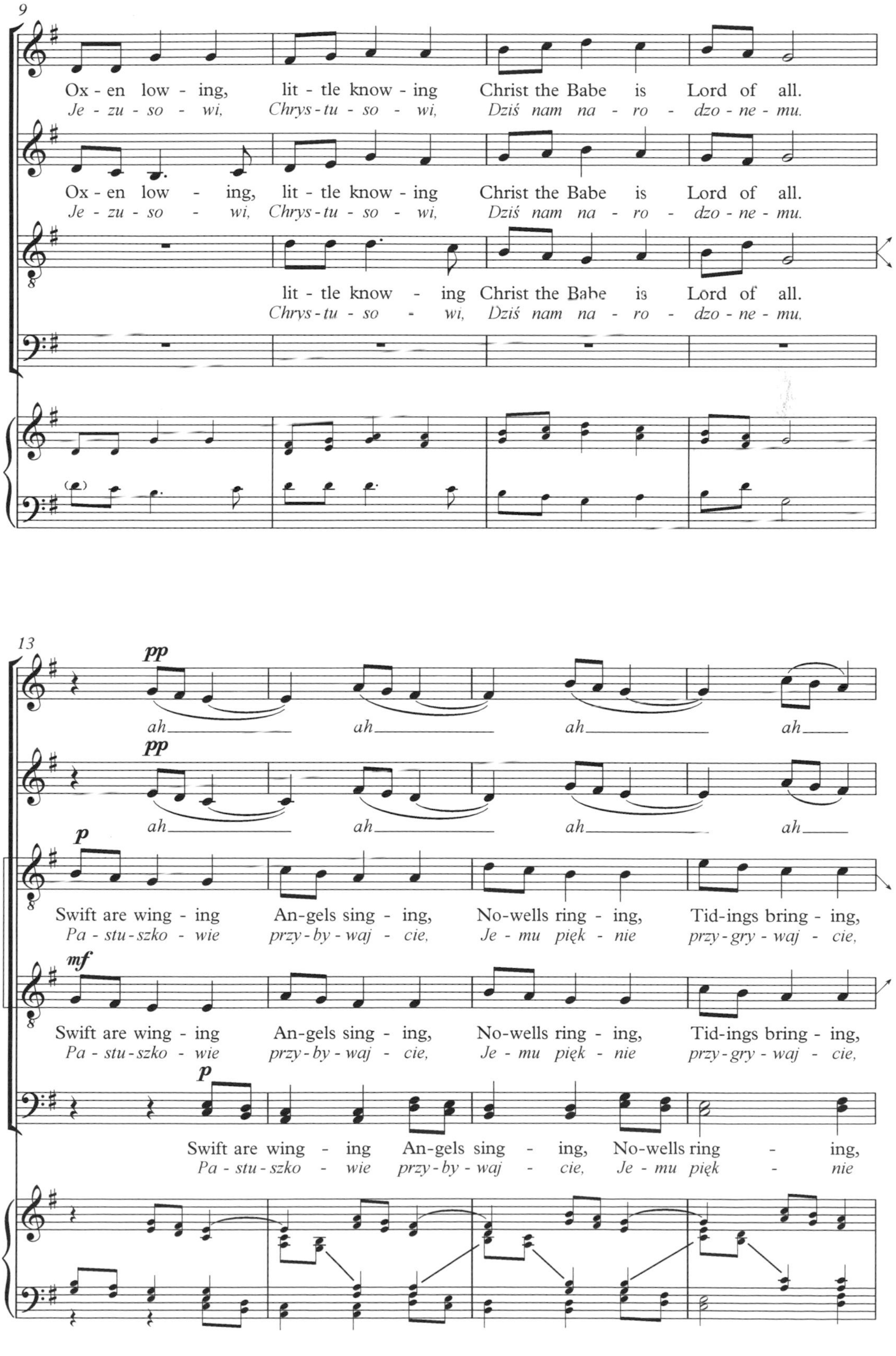

13

pp

ah ah ah ah

pp

ah ah ah ah

p

Swift are wing - ing An-gels sing - ing, No-wells ring - ing, Tid-ings bring - ing,

Pa - stu - szko - wie przy - by - waj - cie, Je - mu pięk - nie przy - gry - waj - cie,

mf

Swift are wing - ing An-gels sing - ing, No-wells ring - ing, Tid-ings bring - ing,

Pa - stu - szko - wie przy - by - waj - cie, Je - mu pięk - nie przy - gry - waj - cie,

p

Swift are wing - ing An-gels sing - ing, No-wells ring - ing,

Pa - stu - szko - wie przy - by - waj - cie, Je - mu pięk - nie

17

mf

Christ the Babe is Lord of all, Christ the Babe is Lord of all.
Ja - ko Pa - nu na - sze - mu, Ja - ko Pa - nu na - sze - mu.

mf

Christ the Babe is Lord of all, Christ the Babe is
Ja - ko Pa - nu na - sze - mu, Ja - ko Pa - nu

mf

Christ the Babe is Lord of all, Christ the Babe is Lord of all.
Ja - ko Pa - nu na - sze - mu, Ja - ko Pa - nu na - sze - mu.

mf

Christ the Babe is Lord of all, Christ the Babe is
Ja - ko Pa - nu na - sze - mu, Ja - ko Pa - nu

21

Lord of all.
na - sze - mu.

Lord of all.
na - sze - mu.

p

Man.

Ped.

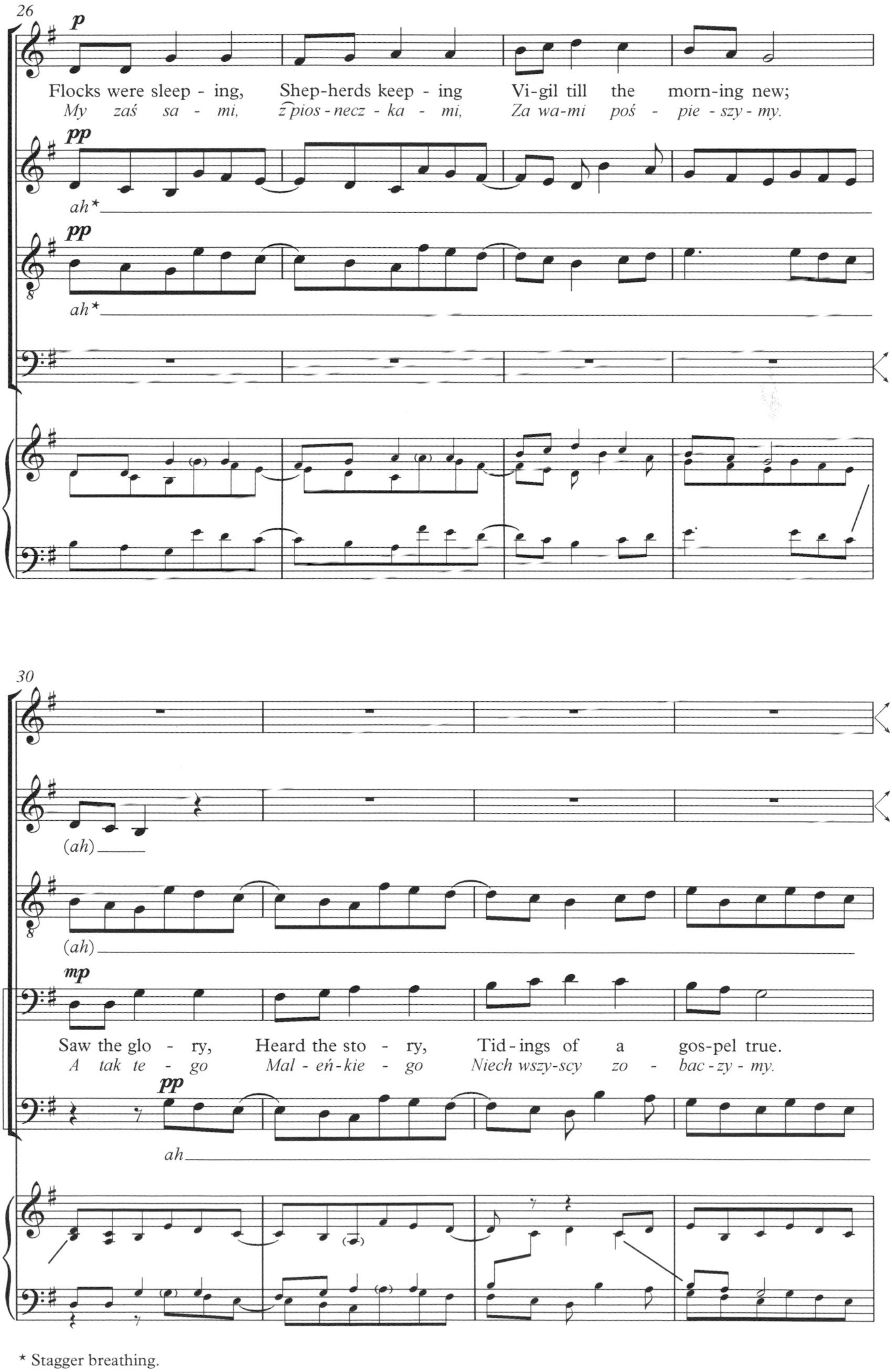

30

(ah)

(ah)

mp

Saw the glo - ry, Heard the sto - ry, Tid-ings of a gos-pel true.

A tak te - go Mal - eń-kie - go Niech wszy-scy zo - bac - zy - my.

pp

ah

* Stagger breathing.

34
mf
ah ah ah ah
f
Thus re-joic - ing, Free from sor - row, Prai-ses voic - ing, Greet the mor - row,
Jak u-bo - go na - rod - zo - ny, Płac - ze w͡staj - ni po - lo - żo - ny
mf
ah ah ah ah
mf
Thus re - joic - ing, Free from sor - row, Prai-ses voic - ing,
Jak u - bo - go na - rod - zo - ny, Płac - ze w͡staj - ni
mf
Thus re-joic - ing, Free from sor - row, Prai-ses voic - ing, Greet the mor - row,
Jak u-bo - go na - rod - zo - ny, Płac - ze w͡staj - ni po - lo - żo - ny
mf
Thus re - joic - ing, Free from sor - row, Prai-ses voic - ing,
Jak u - bo - go na - rod - zo - ny, Płac - ze w͡staj - ni
mf
Thus re - joic - ing, Free from sor - row, Prai-ses voic - ing,
Jak u - bo - go na - rod - zo - ny, Płac - ze w͡staj - ni

38
mp
Christ the Babe was born for you!
Więc go dziś u - cie - szy-my.
mf
ah
mp
Christ the Babe was born for you!
Więc go dziś u - cie - szy-my.
mp
Christ the Babe was born for you!
Więc go dziś u - cie - szy - my.
Christ the Babe was born for you!
Więc go dziś u - cie - szy - my,
mp
Christ the Babe was born for you!
Więc go dziś u - cie - szy - my.
Christ the Babe was born for you!
Więc go dziś u - cie - szy - my,
mp
Christ the Babe was born for you!
Więc go dziś u - cie - szy - my.
mp
Christ the Babe was born for you! for you!
Więc go dziś u - cie - szy - my, u - cie - szy - my.

The infant King

S. Baring-Gould (1834–1924)

Basque noël
arr. David Willcocks (b.1919)

2. *Sing lullaby!*
Lullaby baby, now a-sleeping,
Sing lullaby!
Hush, do not wake the Infant King.
Soon will come sorrow with the morning,
Soon will come bitter grief and weeping:
Sing lullaby!

3. *Sing lullaby!*
Lullaby baby, now a-dozing,
Sing lullaby!
Hush, do not wake the Infant King.
Soon comes the cross, the nails, the piercing,
Then in the grave at last reposing:
Sing lullaby!

4. *Sing lullaby!*
Lullaby! is the babe awaking?
Sing lullaby!
Hush, do not stir the Infant King.
Dreaming of Easter, gladsome morning,
Conquering Death, its bondage breaking:
Sing lullaby!

It came upon the midnight clear

E.H. Sears
(1810–76)

traditional, adapted by Arthur Sullivan
(1842–1900)
verse 4 arr. Stephen Cleobury

9
'Peace on the earth, good - will to men, From heav'n's all - gra - cious King!'
A - bove its sad and low - ly plains They bend on ho - v'ring wing;
And man, at war with man, hears not The love - song which they bring:
'Peace on the earth, good - will to men, From heav'n's all - gra - cious King!'
A - bove its sad and low - ly plains They bend on ho - v'ring wing;
And man, at war with man, hears not The love - song which they bring:
'Peace on the earth, good - will to men, From heav'n's all - gra - cious King!'
A - bove its sad and low - ly plains They bend on ho - v'ring wing;
And man, at war with man, hears not The love - song which they bring:
'Peace on the earth, good - will to men, From heav'n's all - gra - cious King!'
A - bove its sad and low ly plains They bend on ho - v'ring wing;
And man, at war with man, hears not The love - song which they bring:
13
The world in so - lemn still - ness lay To hear the an - gels sing.
And ev - er o'er its Ba - bel sounds The bless - ed an - gels sing.
O hush the noise, ye men of strife, And hear the an - gels sing!
The world in so - lemn still - ness lay To hear the an - gels sing.
And ev - er o'er its Ba - bel sounds The bless - ed an - gels sing.
O hush the noise, ye men of strife, And hear the an - gels sing!
The world in so - lemn still - ness lay To hear the an - gels sing.
And ev - er o'er its Ba - bel sounds The bless - ed an - gels sing.
O hush the noise, ye men of strife, And hear the an - gels sing!
The world in so - lemn still - ness lay To hear the an - gels sing.
And ev - er o'er its Ba - bel sounds The bless - ed an - gels sing.
O hush the noise, ye men of strife, And hear the an - gels sing!

17
4. For lo! the days are hast'-ning on, By_ pro - phet bards fore - told, When
4. For lo! the days are hast'-ning on, By pro - phet bards fore - told, When
4. For lo! the days are hast' - ning on, By_ pro - phet bards fore - told,_____ When
4. For lo! the days are hast' - ning on, By_ pro - phet bards fore - told, When
21
with the e - ver - circ - ling years Comes round the age of gold: When
with the e - ver - circ - ling years Comes round the age of gold: When
with the e - ver - circ - ling years Comes round the age of gold:_____ When
with the e - ver - circ - ling years Comes round the age of gold: When

25
peace shall o - ver all the earth its an-cient splen-dour fling, And
peace shall o - ver all the earth its an-cient splen-dour fling, And
peace shall o - ver all the earth its an - cient splen-dour fling, And
peace shall o - ver all the earth its an-cient splen - dour fling, And
29
the whole world send back the song Which now the an - gels sing.
the whole world send back the song Which now the an - gels sing.
the whole world send back the song Which now the an - gels sing.
the whole world send back the song Which now the an - gels sing.

Jesus Christ the apple tree

New Hampshire, 1784

Elizabeth Poston (1905–87)

1. The tree of life my soul hath seen,
Laden with fruit, and always green:
The trees of nature fruitless be
Compared with Christ the apple tree.

2. His beauty doth all things excel:
By faith I know, but ne'er can tell
The glory which I now can see
In Jesus Christ the apple tree.

3. For happiness I long have sought,
And pleasure dearly I have bought:
I missed of all; but now I see
'Tis found in Christ the apple tree.

4. I'm weary with my former toil,
Here I will sit and rest awhile:
Under the shadow I will be,
Of Jesus Christ the apple tree.

5. This fruit doth make my soul to thrive,
It keeps my dying faith alive;
Which makes my soul in haste to be
With Jesus Christ the apple tree.

for Simon's 3rd birthday

The Lamb

William Blake
(1757–1827)

John Tavener
(b.1944)

With extreme tenderness – flexible – always guided by the words (♩ = c. 40)

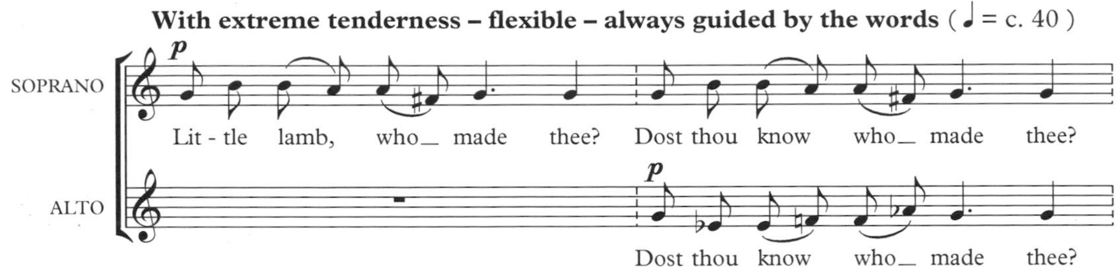

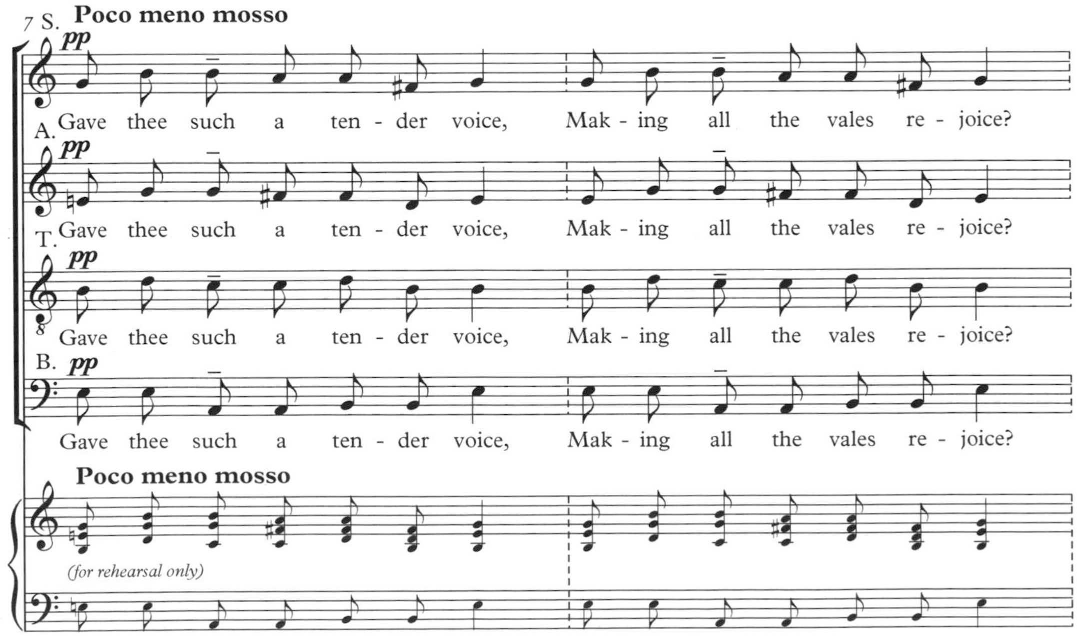

9
Lit-tle Lamb, who made thee? Dost thou know who made thee?
Lit-tle Lamb, who made thee? Dost thou know who made thee?
Lit-tle Lamb who made thee? Dost thou know who made thee?
Lit-tle Lamb who made thee? Dost thou know who made thee?

11
a tempo – moving forward
mp
Lit-tle Lamb, I'll tell thee, Lit-tle Lamb, I'll tell thee;
mp
Lit-tle Lamb, I'll tell thee, Lit-tle Lamb, I'll tell thee;
mp
Lit-tle Lamb, I'll tell thee, Lit-tle Lamb, I'll tell thee;
mp
Lit-tle Lamb, I'll tell thee, Lit-tle Lamb, I'll tell thee;
a tempo – moving forward

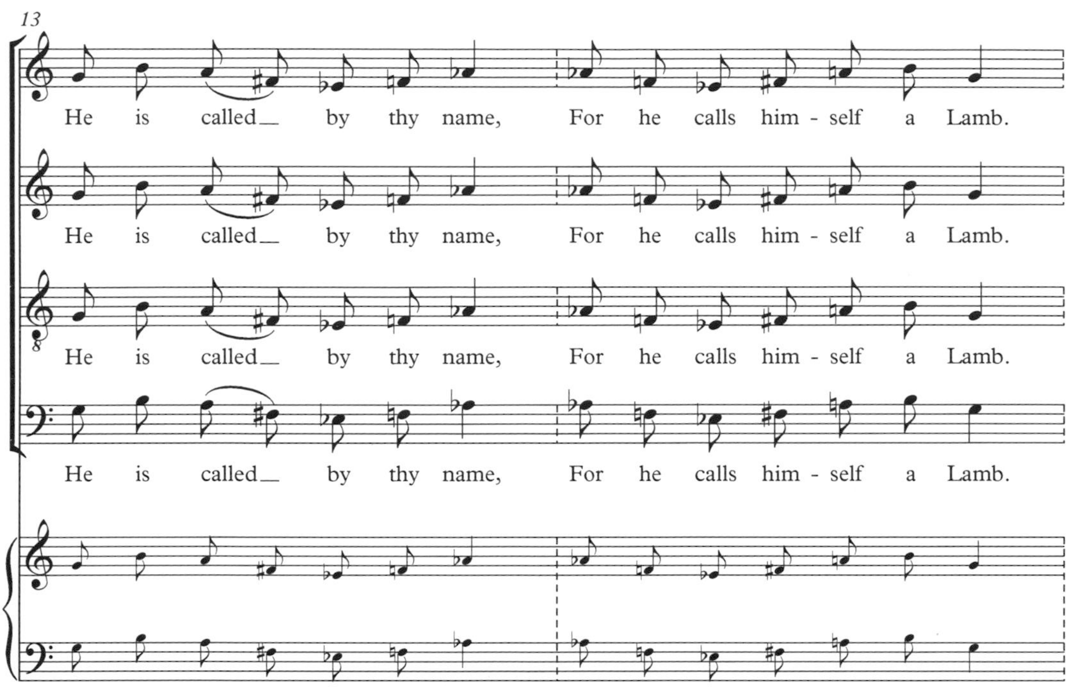
13
He is called_ by thy name, For he calls him - self a Lamb.
He is called_ by thy name, For he calls him - self a Lamb.
He is called_ by thy name, For he calls him - self a Lamb.
He is called_ by thy name, For he calls him - self a Lamb.

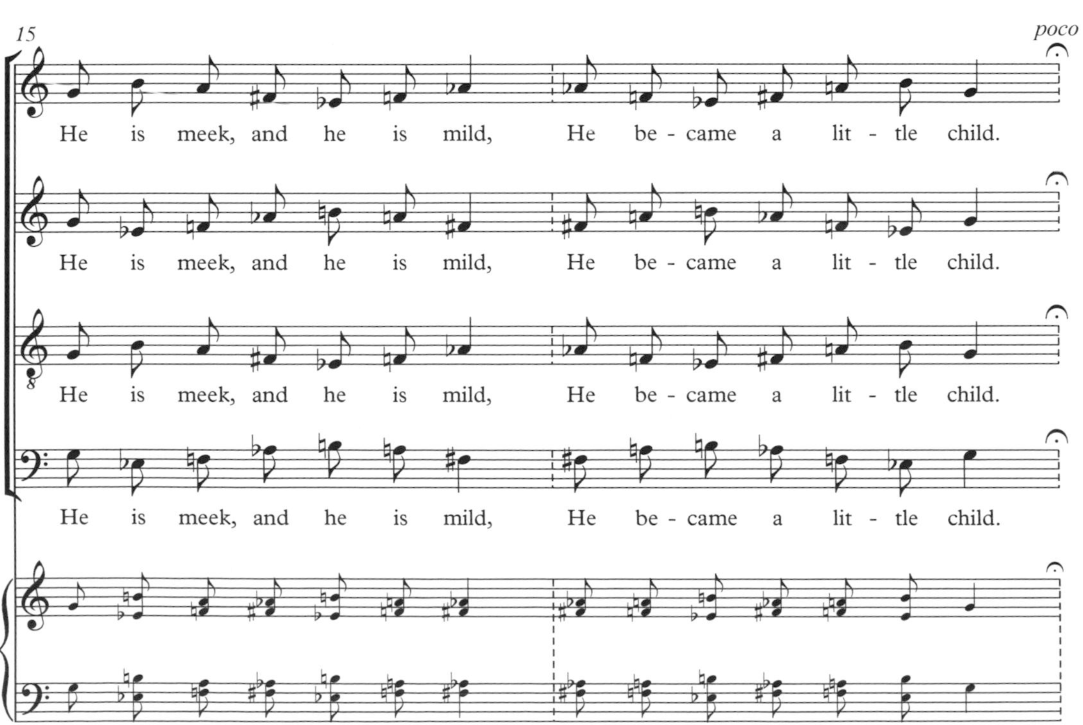
15
poco
He is meek, and he is mild, He be - came a lit - tle child.
He is meek, and he is mild, He be - came a lit - tle child.
He is meek, and he is mild, He be - came a lit - tle child.
He is meek, and he is mild, He be - came a lit - tle child.

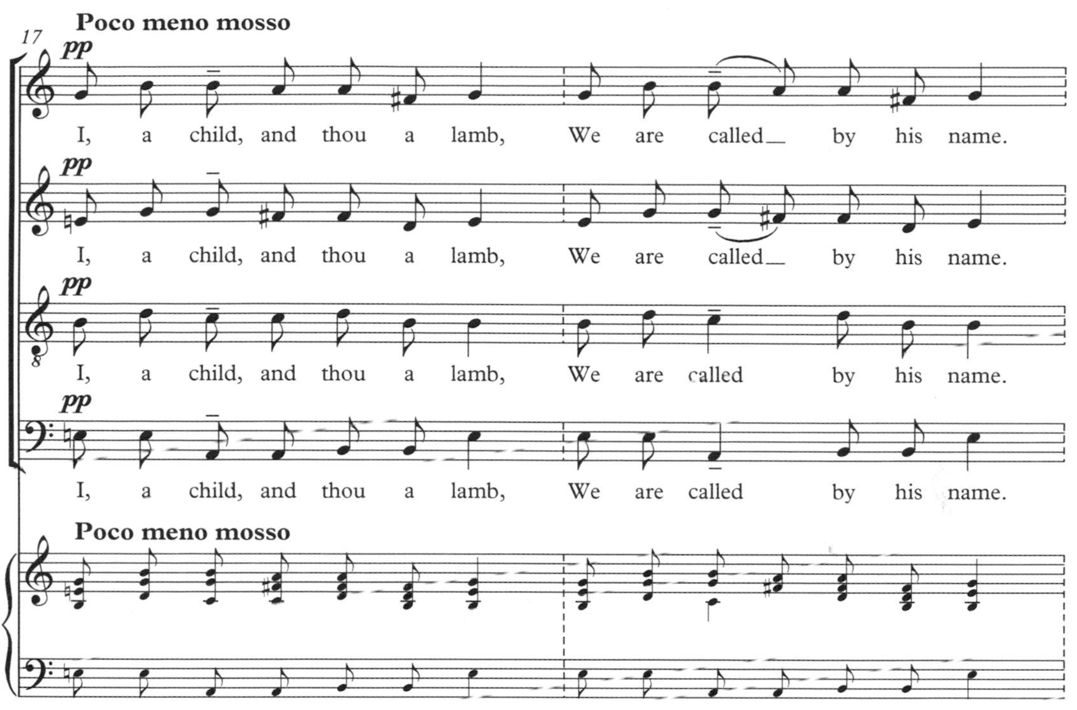
17
Poco meno mosso
pp
I, a child, and thou a lamb, We are called by his name.
Poco meno mosso

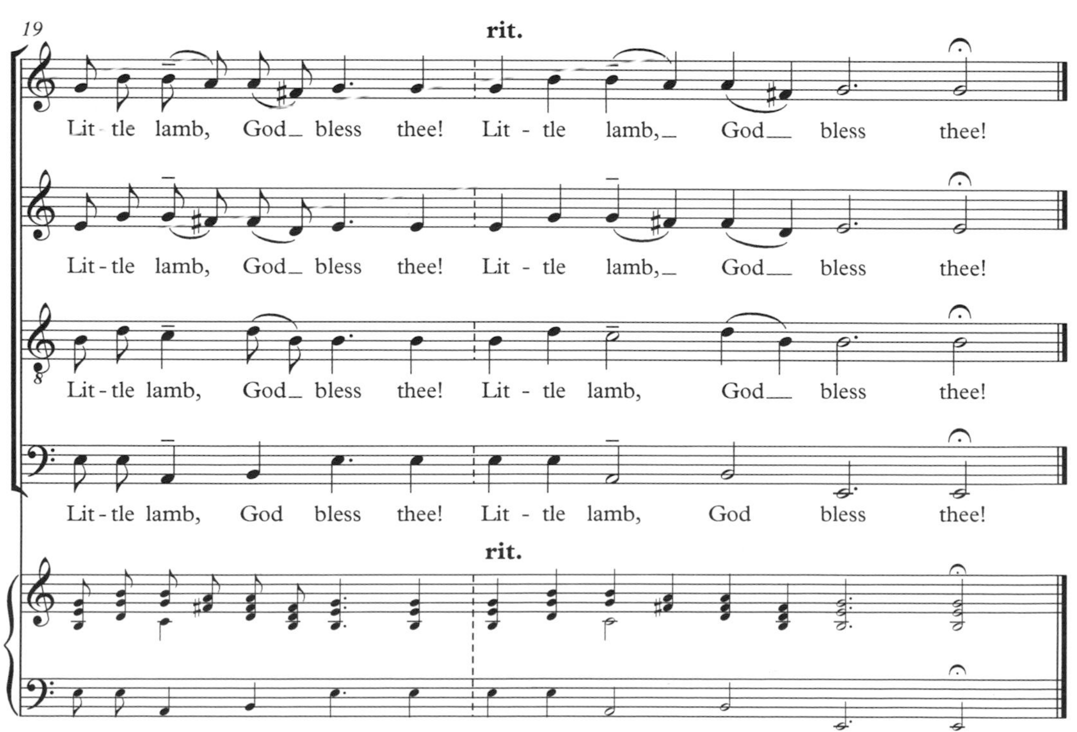
19
rit.
Lit-tle lamb, God bless thee! Lit - tle lamb, God bless thee!
rit.

Morning song for the Christ Child

Roger Covell
(b.1931)

Peter Sculthorpe
(b.1929)

8

1. poco rall.

cresc.

-gain, gone___ and ne - ver found a - gain. Ah___
hurt, old___ and deep and past all hurt. Ah_

cresc.

___ la___ la___

cresc.

___ la___ la___

cresc.

___ la la la la___ la la la___ la

1. poco rall.

12

2. molto rall.

a tempo, ma accel. poco a poco

mf *(cresc.)* *mf* *pp* *molto cresc.*

___ (ah)___ La la (or Mm)___

mf *(cresc.)* *mf* *pp molto cresc.*

la la___ la___ la la___ La la (or Mm)___

mf *(cresc.)* *mf*

la la___ la___ la la___

mf *(cresc.)* *mf*

la la la la la___ la la la la

2. molto rall.

a tempo, ma accel. poco a poco

17

(molto cresc.)

a tempo

ff

Ah

(molto cresc.)

ff

la

mf molto cresc.

ff

La la la la

la

mf molto cresc.

ff

La la la la

la la la

a tempo

24

mf teneramente

3. Green morn-ing sleeps, the sky is sown, Kind and calm and all a-

mf sub.

la la

mf sub.

la la

mf sub. mp mf

la la la la la la la la la la la

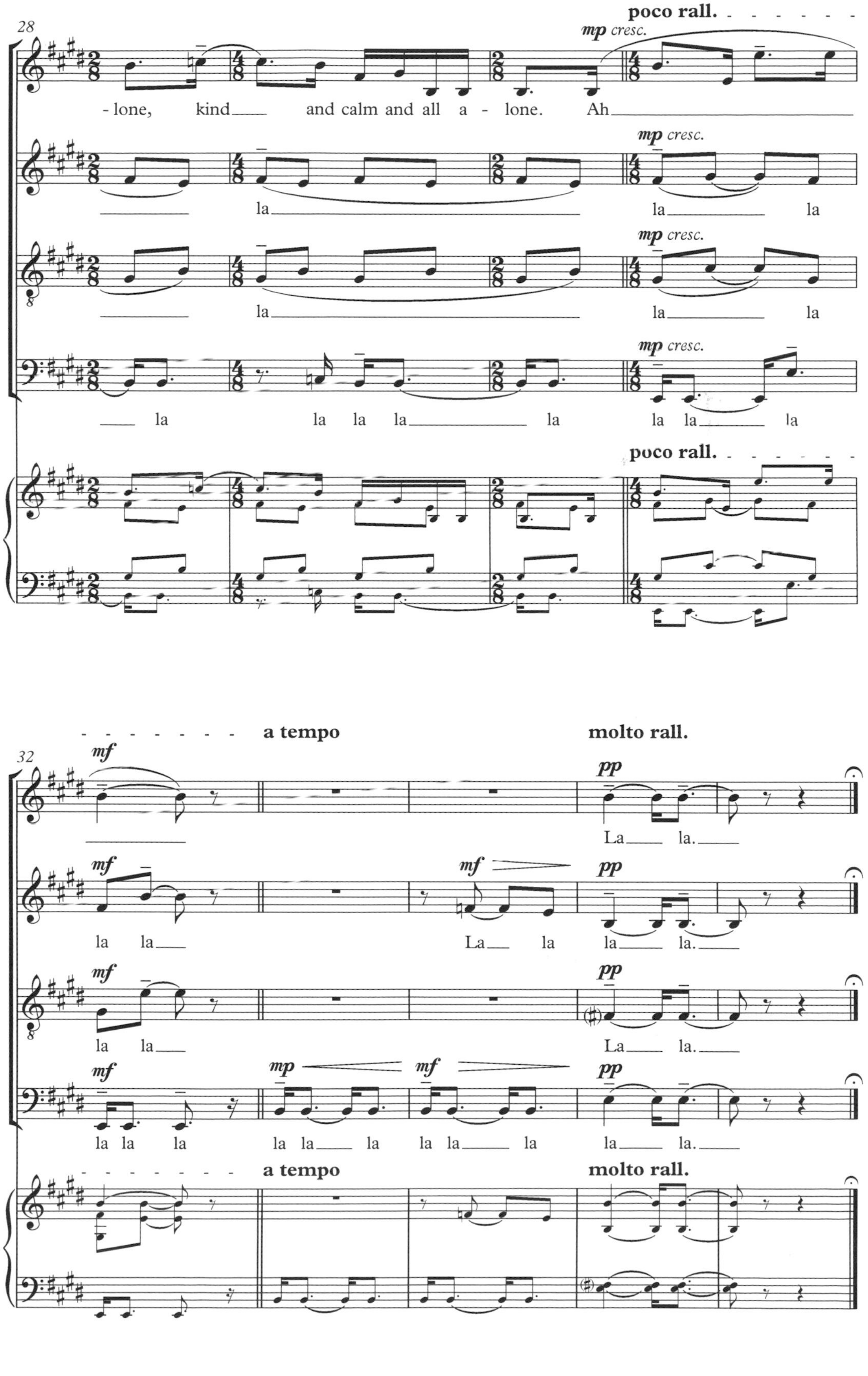

poco rall.

28

mp cresc.

- lone, kind and calm and all a - lone. Ah

mp cresc.

la la la

mp cresc.

la la la

mp cresc.

la la la la la la la la

poco rall.

Myn lyking

15th century

R.R. Terry (1865–1938)

In the original of verses 2 & 3, the four quavers before the final minim have tenuto marks.

Order of performance: verse 1, bars 1-12; verse 2, repeat bars 1-12; verse 3, bars 13-20 and 9-12; verse 4, bars 13-20 and 9-16.

No small wonder

Paul Wigmore (b.1925)

Paul Edwards (b.1956)

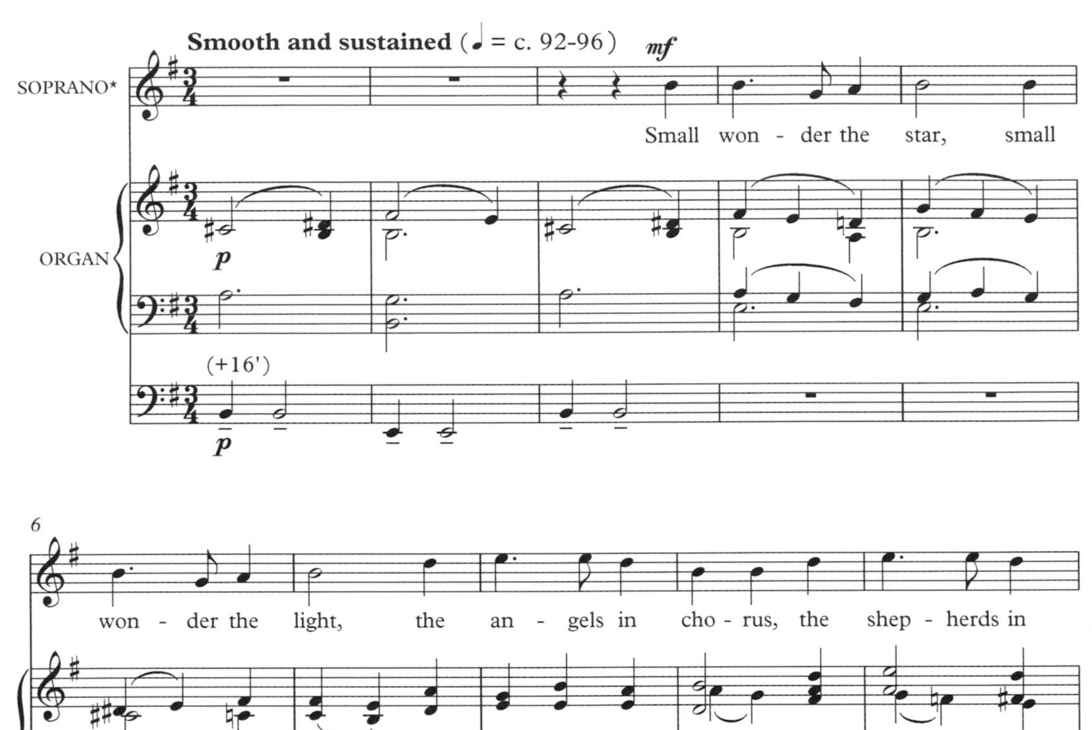

* May be sung by a soloist to bar 16.

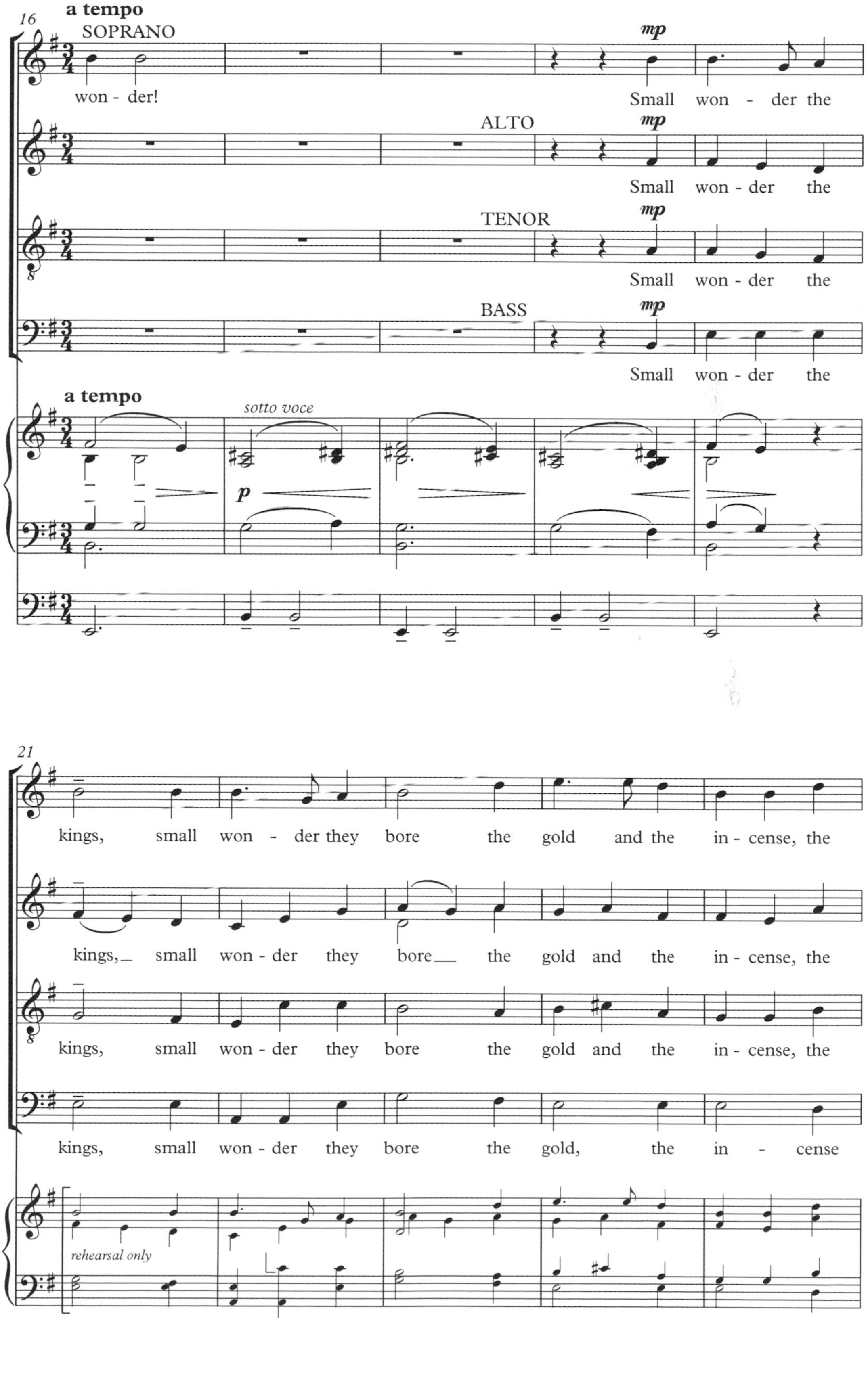

16

a tempo

SOPRANO

mp

won - der! Small won - der the

ALTO

mp

Small won - der the

TENOR

mp

Small won - der the

BASS

mp

Small won - der the

a tempo

sotto voce

p

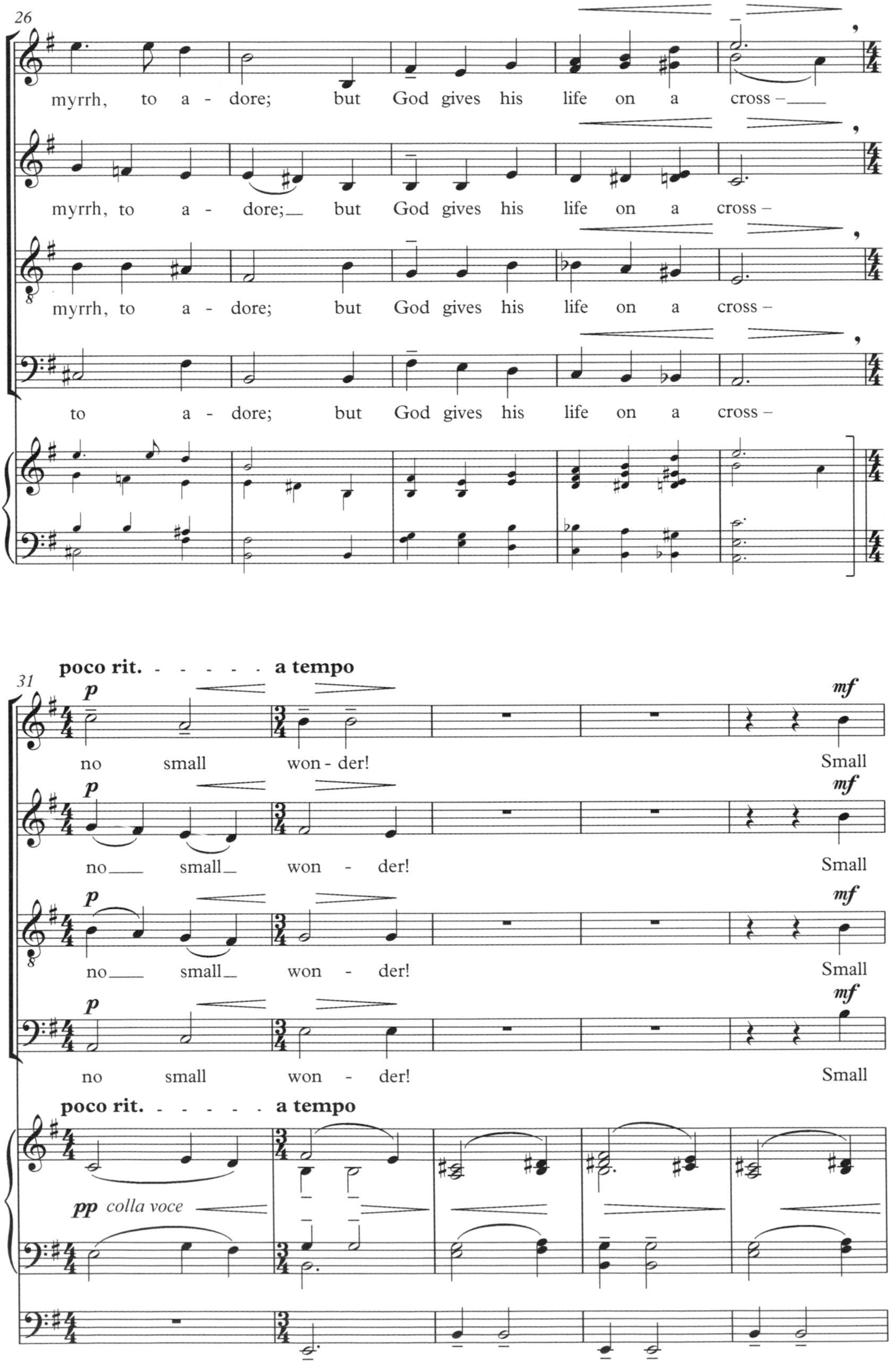

31

poco rit. - - - - - **a tempo**

p no small won - der! *mf* Small

p no small won - der! *mf* Small

p no small won - der! *mf* Small

p no small won - der! *mf* Small

poco rit. - - - - - **a tempo**

pp colla voce

36
poco a poco cresc.
won - der the love, small won - der the grace, the pow - er, the
poco a poco cresc.
won - der the love, small won - der the grace, the pow - er, the
poco a poco cresc.
won - der the love, small won - der the grace, the pow - er, the
poco a poco cresc.
won - der the love, small won - der the grace, the glo -
mf
poco a poco cresc.
41
f
allarg.
a tempo
mp
glo - ry, the light of his face; but all to re -
f
mp
glo - ry, the light of his face; but all to re -
f
mp
glo - ry, the light of his face; but all to re -
f
mp
- ry, the light of his face; but all to re -
allarg.
a tempo
f

rall. molto rall. a tempo

45

mp

-deem my poor heart – no small won - der!

mp

-deem my poor heart – no small won - der!

mp

-deem my poor heart – no small won - der!

mp

-deem my poor heart – no small won - der!

rall. molto rall. a tempo

p

Love came down at Christmas

Christina Rossetti (1830–94)

R.O. Morris (1886–1948)

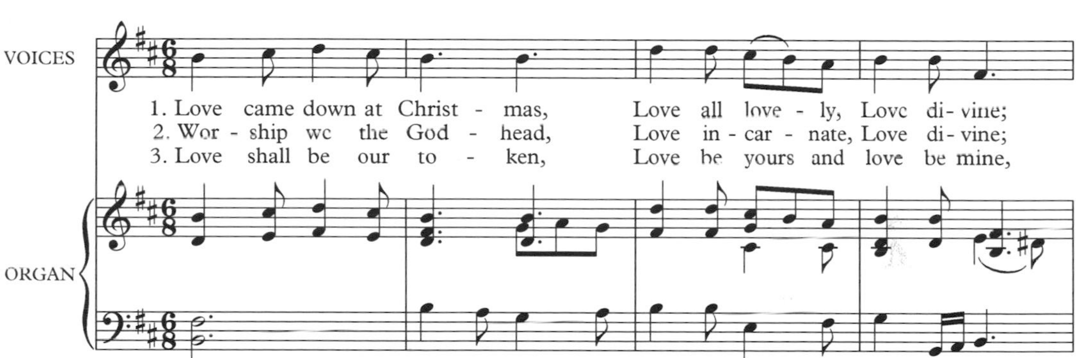

The verses may be sung by varying combinations of voices, eg:
v.1 tenors and basses;
v.2 trebles/sopranos;
v.3 full.

for the choir of St. Peter ad Vincula, H.M. Tower of London

Noël nouvelet

English words by
Marion Jackson
(b.1921)

French traditional
arr. Stephen Jackson
(b.1951)

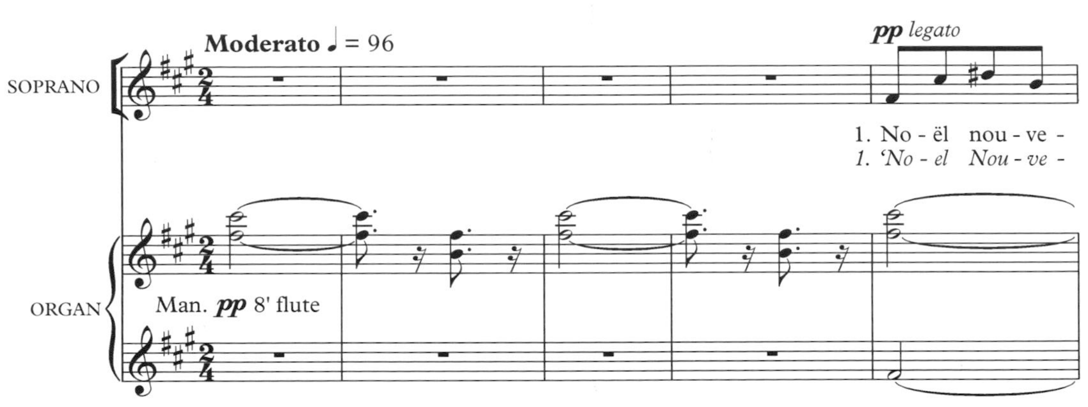

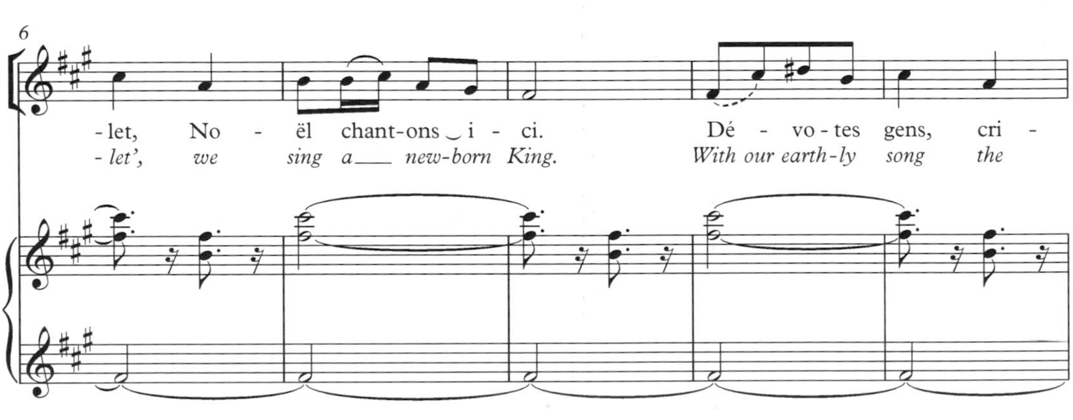

17
No-ël nou-ve-let, No - ël chant-ons ‿ i - ci.
'No-el Nou-ve-let' for Christ the new-born King.
23
29
TENORS
p
2. L'an - ge dis-ait: 'Pas - teurs, par - tez d'i - ci,
2. 'Shep-herds from the fields, let glad-ness fill your mind.
p (strings)
Ped. 16' only
35
L'â-me en re-pos et le coeur ré-jou - i;
Go to Beth-le - hem, the Lamb of God to find!'
En Beth-lé - em* trou-
Lo, from the sky the

* Bett-lé-emm

* Pronounce 's' in 'tous'.

56
mm,
-fant, Jo - seph, Ma - rie aus - si. La crèche é - tait au
found Jo - seph and Ma - ry there. With them they mar - velled
-vent l'en - fant, Jo - seph, Ma - rie aus - si. La crèche é - tait
haste and found Jo seph and Ma - ry there. With them they mar -
mm,
61
mm,
lieu d'un ber - ce - let. No - ël nou - ve - let, No - ël chant - ons i -
at this ho - ly thing: 'No - el Nou - ve - let' for Christ the new - born
au lieu d'un ber - ce - let. No - ël nou - ve - let, No - ël chant -
- velled at this ho - ly thing: 'No - el Nou - ve - let' for Christ the
mm,

66
- ci.
King.
-tons i - ci.
new-born King.
p
Ped. 8 ' & 16 '
mf
72
sf mf sonore
Mm,
sf mf sonore
Mm,
sf mf sonore
Mm,
mf
4. Bien - tôt les rois, par l'é-toile é - clair - cis,
4. Soon the three wise men, who by a star were led,
Solo
(Ped.)

78
sf mf
mm,
sf mf
mm,
sf mf
mm,
sf mf
mm,
sf mf
mm,
sf mf
mm,
De l'O - rient dont ils é - taient sor - tis, A Beth - lé -
Jour-neyed from the East, and at the low - ly bed Each bowed the
83
sf mf
mm,
sf mf
mm,
sf mf
mm,
-em vin - rent un ma - ti - net. No - ël nou-ve - let, No -
knee and made an of - fer - ing: 'No - el Nou ve - let' to

88
-ël chant-ons ‿ i - ci.
Christ the new-born King.
p
93
rall.
rall.
(Man.)
p

* 'st' not pronounced

104
pp
pro - dige ac - com - pli De nous sau - ver par son sang ver - meil-
borne my grief and pain, Bring - ing me heal - ing through Thy suf - fer -
ac - com - pli De nous sau - ver par son sang
borne my pain, Bring - ing me heal - ing through Thy
ac - com - pli De nous sau - ver par son
borne my pain, Bring - ing heal - ing, through thy
ac - com - pli De nous sau - ver par
borne my pain, Bring - ing heal - ing
- ra le pro - dige ac - com - pli De nous sau -
Cross hast borne my grief and pain, Bring - ing heal -

109
cresc.
Ah,
cresc.
- let! No - ël nou - ve - let, No - ël chant-ons i - ci.
- ing. 'No - el Nou - ve - let' for Christ the heav'n-ly King.
mp
ver - meil - let! No - ël, No - ël, son
suf - fer - ing. 'No - el, no - el' the
mp
sang! No - ël, No - ël, son
suf - fer - ing. 'No - el, No - el,' the
mp
son sang ver - meil - let! No - ël son
through Thy suf - fer - ing, 'No - el' the
- ver, No - ël, No - ël,
- ing, 'No - el, no - el'

114
sf
sang ver - meil - let!
hea - ven - ly King.
sang ver - meil - let!
hea - ven - ly King.
sang ver - meil - let!
hea - ven - ly King.
ver - meil - let!
heav'n - ly King.
Solo mf
p
8' & 16'
mp

120
poco accel. . . . . Tempo I
pp
No-ël nou-ve - let, No -
'No-el Nou-ve - let', we
poco accel. . . . . Tempo I
ff
pp
127
S.
-ël chant-ons i - ci. Dé - vo-tes gens, cri - ons à Dieu mer-
sing a new-born King. With our earth-ly song the firm-a - ment shall

132
poco cresc.
pp sub.
- ci! Chant-ons No - ël pour le roi nou-ve - let. No - ël nou-ve -
ring. See how the love of God such joy doth bring. 'No - el Nou-ve -
16' off
138
- let, No - ël chant-ons ‿ i - ci.
- let' for Christ the new-born King.
143
rit.
8' only
149
Meno mosso
pp possibile
add 16'

for the Choir of King's College, Cambridge

Nowel

Walter de la Mare
(1873–1956)

Richard Rodney Bennett
(b.1936)

Moderato giocoso ♩ = 72 **(sempre molto ritmico)**

SOPRANO

ALTO

f

No-wel, no-wel, No-wel, no - wel, No-wel, no-wel,

TENOR

BASS

f

No-wel, no-wel, No-wel, no - wel, No-wel, no-wel,

Moderato giocoso ♩ = 72 **(sempre molto ritmico)**

PIANO
(for rehearsal only)

5

f largamente

Ho-ly dark: pale Mis-tle - toe,

No-wel, no - wel, No-wel, no-wel, No-wel, no - wel,

f largamente

Ho-ly dark: pale Mis-tle - toe,

No-wel, no - wel, No-wel, no-wel, No-wel, no - wel,

Text by Walter de la Mare reproduced by permission of The Literary Trustees of Walter de la Mare and The Society of Authors as their representative.

10
Christ - mas eve is come, and lo, Wild clash the bells a -
No - wel, no - wel, No - wel, no - wel, No - wel, no - wel, No - wel, no -
Christ - mas eve is come, and lo, Wild clash the bells a -
No - wel, no - wel, No - wel, no - wel, No - wel, no - wel, No - wel, no -
15
(f sempre)
cross the snow, Waits in the dark streets ca - rol - ling go;
wel, No - wel, no - wel, No - wel, no - wel,
cross the snow, Waits in the dark streets ca - rol - ling go;
wel, No - wel, no - wel, No - wel, no - wel,

19
ff appassionato
'No-wel! No-wel!' they shout and oh, How
No-wel, no-wel, No-wel, no-wel, oh, How
Now-wel, no-wel, No-wel, no-wel, oh, How
24
live out the day!
mp espressivo
Each breath I breathe turns
No-wel, no-wel No-wel, no-
Each breath I breathe turns

29
to a sigh; My heart is flown a - way; No-wel, no-wel, No-
-wel, No-wel, no-wel, No-wel, no-wel, The things I
-wel, No-wel, no-wel, No-wel, no-wel, The things I
to a sigh; My heart is flown a - way; No-wel, no-wel, No-
34
poco cresc.
-wel, no - wel, No-wel, no - wel, No - wel, no - wel,
see a - round me seem En - tranced with light as in a
see a - round me seem En - tranced with light as in a
-wel, no - wel, No-wel, no - wel, No - wel, no - wel,

38
mf
The can-dles daz-zle in my eyes, And
dream; No-wel, no-wel, No-wel, no-wel, No-wel,
dream; No-wel, no-wel, No-wel, no-wel, No-wel,
The can-dles daz-zle in my eyes, And
42
cresc.
ev-'ry leap-ing fire-flame tries To sing what none could say.
no-wel, No-wel, no-wel, No-wel, no-wel, No-
no-wel, No-wel, no-wel, No-wel, no-wel, No-
ev-'ry leap-ing fire-flame tries To sing what none could say.

46
ff
Nowel, nowel, nowel, nowel, Nowel, nowel,
-wel, nowel, Nowel, nowel, nowel, nowel, Nowel, nowel,
-wel, nowel, No - wel, nowel, nowel, nowel, No - wel,
No - wel, nowel, nowel, nowel, No - wel,
51
fff
nowel, nowel, Nowel, nowel, no - wel!
nowel, nowel, Nowel, nowel, no - wel!
nowel, nowel, nowel, No - wel, nowel, no - wel!
nowel, nowel, nowel, No - wel, nowel, no - wel!

The truth sent from above

(The Herefordshire Christmas Carol)

English traditional
arr. R. Vaughan Williams
(1872–1958)

Verse 1 may be sung by a solo voice

O little town of Bethlehem (I)

Bishop Phillips Brooks (1835–93)

traditional, arr. R. Vaughan Williams (1872–1958)
verse 4 arr. Stephen Cleobury

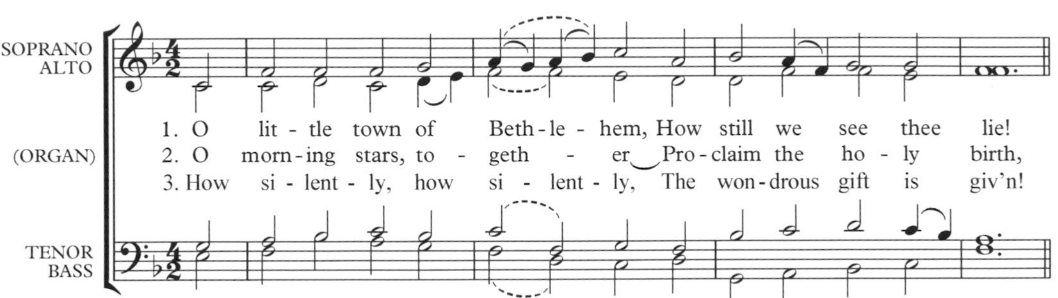

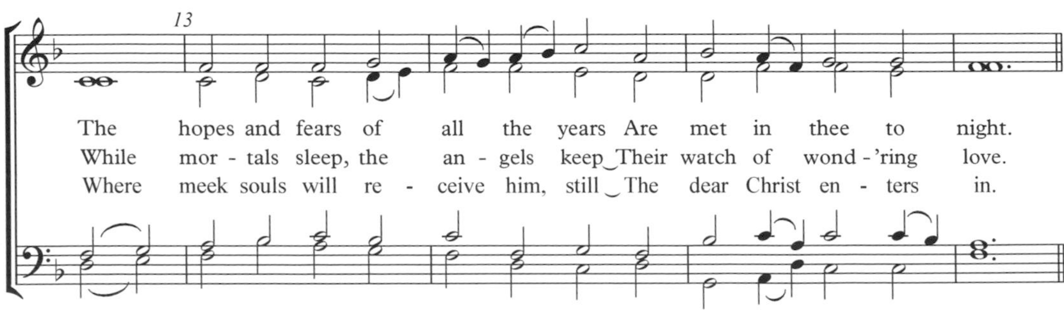

[CONGREGATION: SING TENOR LINE.]

22

en - ter__ in, Be born in us__ to - day.

en - ter__ in, Be born in us to - day.________

en - ter__ in, Be born in__ us to - day. We__

en - ter in, Be born in us to - day.

25

We hear the Christ-mas an - - gels The

The Christ - mas an - - gels The

hear the Christ - mas__ an - - gels The

The Christ - mas an - - - gels The

27
great glad tid - ings tell: O__ come to us, a - bide with
great glad tid - ings tell: O__ come to us, a -
great glad tid - ings tell: O come to us, a -
great glad tid - ings tell: O__ come to us, a -
30
us,__ Our Lord Em - ma - nu - el.
-bide with us, Our Lord Em - ma - nu - el.
- bide__ with__ us, Our Lord Em - ma - nu - el.
-bide with us, Our Lord Em - ma - nu - el.

O little town of Bethlehem (II)

Bishop Phillips Brooks (1835–93)

Henry Walford Davies (1869–1941)

15
Allegretto semplice
TUTTI
mp
O lit - tle town of Beth - le - hem, How
mp
p
con Ped.
20
(poco rit.)
(a tempo)
still we see thee lie! A - bove thy deep and dream-less sleep, The
(poco rit.)
(a tempo)
24
mf
cresc.
si - lent stars go by: Yet in thy dark streets shin - eth The
mf
cresc.
Ped.
Ped.
28
f
e - ver - last - ing light; The hopes and fears of all the years Are
f
etc.

rit. - - - - - - a tempo
Poco meno mosso
pp
met in thee to - night. How
p
Ped.
si - lent - ly, how si - lent - ly the won - drous gift is given! So God im - parts to
hu - man hearts The bless - ings of His heaven. No ear may hear His com - ing; But
pp sempre
(rit. e dim.)
(a tempo)
mp
in this world of sin, Where meek souls will re - ceive Him still, The
f
p (a tempo)

51
dim.
(p)
dear Christ en - ters in.
dim.
p
Poco sostenuto
p
56
O ho-ly Child of Beth-le-hem, Des-cend to us we pray; Cast out our sin, and
p
61
sempre cresc.
en-ter in, Be born in us to-day! We hear the Christ-mas
sempre cresc.
65
f
ff
an - gels The great glad tid-ings tell; O, come to us a - bide with us, Our
f
ff
70
p
Lord Em-man - - u - el!
p
p

Of the Father's heart begotten

Prudentius (b. 348)
tr. R.F. Davis (1866–1937)

melody from *Piae Cantiones*
arr. Stephen Cleobury

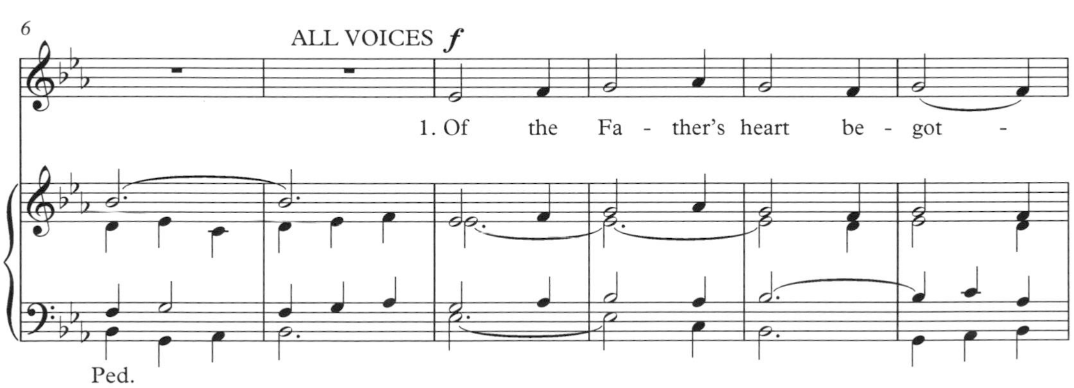

19
from that Foun - tain All that is and hath been
25
flows; He is O - me - ga, of all
31
things Yet to come the mys - tic Close, Ev - er -
37
-more and ev - er - more.

43
SOPRANOS and ALTOS
p
2. By his word was all cre - a - ted; He com-man - ded and 'twas done;
4. O how blest that won-drous birth - day, When the Maid the curse re-trieved,
p
52
Earth and sky and bound-less o - cean, U - ni-verse of three in one,
Brought to birth man-kind's sal - va - tion, By the Ho - ly Ghost con-ceived;
61
All that sees the moon's soft ra - - diance, All that breathes be -
And the Babe, the world's Re - deem - - er, In her lov - ing
69
-neath the sun,
arms re-ceived,
Ev - er-more and ev - er - more.
v.2 to v.3
v.4 to v.5

TENORS and BASSES
78
f
3. He as-sumed this mor - tal bo - dy, Frail and fee - ble, doomed to die,
5. This is he, whom seer and sy - bil Sang in a - ges long_ gone by;
f
87
That the race from dust cre - a - ted Might not pe - rish ut - ter - ly,
This is he of old re - veal - èd In the page of pro - phe - cy;
96
Which the dread - ful Law had sen - tenced In the depths of hell to lie,
Lo! he comes, the pro - mised Sa - viour; Let the world his prais - es cry!
106
back to v.4
on to v.6
Ev - er - more and ev - er - more.
back to v.4
on to v.6
cresc.

ALL VOICES
113
ff
6. Sing ye heights of heav'n his prais - es; An - gels and Arch - an - gels sing!
ff
122
Where - so - e'er ye be, ye faith - ful, Let your joy - ous an - thems ring, Ev - 'ry
132
tongue his name con - fess - - ing, Count - less voi - ces an - swer - ing,
141
Ev - er - more and ev - er - more.
(Optional)
S.
A.
A - men.
T.
B.

On Christmas night all Christians sing

(*The Sussex Carol*)

English traditional
arr. Philip Ledger (b.1937)

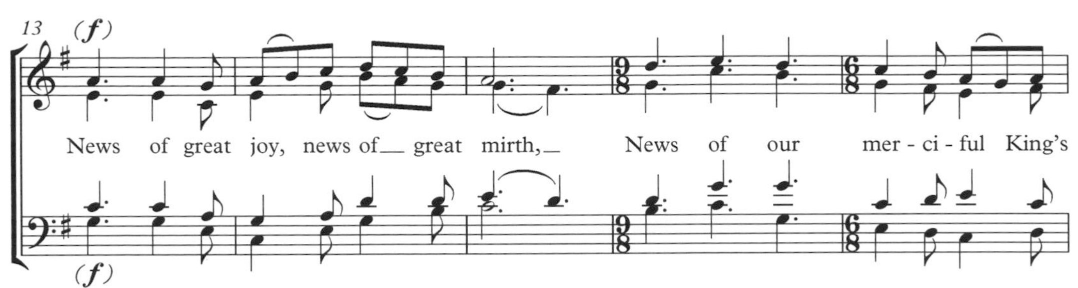
(f)
News of great joy, news of — great mirth, — News of our mer - ci - ful King's
(f)

birth.
birth.
2. Then
mf
mf
mp

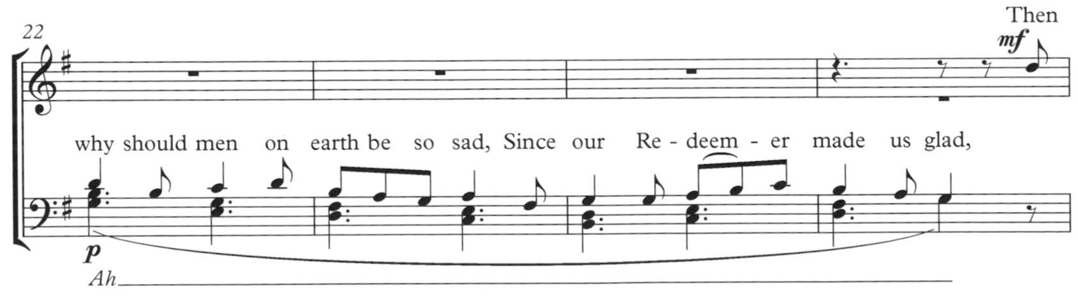
Then
mf
why should men on earth be so sad, Since our Re - deem - er made us glad,
p
Ah

why should men on earth be so sad, Since our Re - deem - er made us glad,
p
Ah

30
mp
When from our sin he set us free,
All for to gain our li - ber-
mp
35
- ty?
p
CHOIR 1 3. When
p
mf
mp
39
CHOIR 1 (TUTTI)
sin de-parts be - fore his grace, then life and health come in its place; When
mf
CHOIR 2
p
sin de - parts be - fore his grace,
p
43
sin de-parts be - fore his grace, then life and health come in its place;
mf
life and health come in its place;
mf

47
cresc.
f
An - gels and men with joy may sing, All for to see the new-born
cresc.
An - gels may sing, All for to see the
cresc.
f
52
ff
King.
4. All
King.
4. All
ff
Add Reeds f
56
CHOIRS 1 & 2 (TUTTI)
out of dark - ness we have light, Which made the an - gels sing this night: All
ff

60
out of dark - ness we have light, Which made the an - gels sing this night:
64
'Glo - ry to God and peace to men, Now and for ev - er - more,
ff
70
senza rall.
ev - er - more. A - men'.
senza rall.
Ped. Reed

Šai svētā naktī

(*On this holy night*)

Valda Mora (1902–2001)
tr. Mara Kalnins (b.1945)

Latvian melody, composer unknown
arr. Stephen Cleobury

6
poco f
mf
-jas Un ien - aids rimst cits ci - tu at - kal mī - ļo
- mune. And en - mi - ty fades, each loves_ the_ o - ther,
-jas Un ien - aids rimst cits ci - tu at - kal mī - ļo
- mune. And en - mi - ty fades, each loves_ the_ o - ther,
-jas Un ien - aids rimst cits_ ci - tu at - kal mī - ļo
- mune. And en - mi - ty fades, each_ loves_ the_ o - ther,
-jas Un ien - aids_ rimst cits ci - tu at - kal mī - ļo
- mune. And en - mi - ty_ fades, each loves_ the_ o - ther,
9
p
Par vi - su mie - ra sil - tie spār - ni klā - jas.
And o'er_ the_ still - ness warm wings ho - ver.
Par vi - su mie - ra sil - tie spār - ni klā - jas.
And o'er_ the_ still - ness warm wings ho - ver.
Par vi - su mie - ra sil - tie spār - ni klā - jas.
And o'er_ the still - ness warm_ wings ho - ver.
Par vi - su mie - ra sil - tie spār - ni klā - jas.
And o'er_ the_ still - ness warm wings_ ho - ver.

12
2. Šai nak - tī e - jot zai - go ta - vas pē -
2. On this night your foot - steps glim -
2. Šai nak - tī e - jot zai - go ta - vas pē -
2. On this night your foot - steps glim -
2. Šai nak - tī e - jot zai - go ta - vas pē -
2. On this night your foot - steps glim -
2. Šai nak - tī e - jot zai - go ta - vas pē -
2. On this night your foot - - steps
14
- das; Šī nakts spēj šau - bas ce - rī - bus tev ie -
- mer, This night trans - fi - gures doubt to
- das; Šī nakts spēj šau - bas ce - rī - bus tev ie -
- - mer, This night trans - fi - gures doubt to
- das; Šī nakts spēj šau - bas ce - rī - bus tev ie -
- mer, This night trans - fi - gures doubt to
- das; Šī nakts spēj šau - bas ce - rī - bus tev ie -
glim - mer, This night trans - fi - gures doubt to

17
mf
- dot; Šī nakts liek aiz - mirst vi - sas bē - das
hope; This night must ban - ish ev - ery sor - row,
mf
- dot; Šī nakts liek aiz - mirst vi - sas bē - das Un
hope; This night must ban - ish ev - ery sor -
(f)
- dot; Šī nakts liek aiz - mirst vi - sas bē - das
hope; This night must ban - ish ev - ery sor - row,
mf
- dot; Šī nakts liek aiz - mirst vi - sas bē - das Un
hope; This night must ban - ish ev - ery sor - row, and
20
mp
Un mā - ca te - vi mī - ļot vi - su pie - dot.
and teach you to for - give and hope.
mp
mā - ca te - vi mī - ļot vi - su pie - dot.
- row, And teach you to for - give and hope.
mf
Un mā - ca te - vi mī - ļot vi - su pie - dot.
and teach you to for - give and hope.
mp
mā - ca te - vi mī - ļot vi - su pie - dot.
teach you to for - give and hope.

S.1
23
mp
3. Šai svē - tā nak - tī,
3. in this ho - ly night,
S.2
p
3. Šai svē - tā nak - tī,
3. On this ho - ly night,
Šai
On this
A.1
mp
3. svē - tā nak - tī,
3. in this ho - ly night,
A.2
p
3. Šai svē - tā nak - tī,
3. On this ho - ly night,
Šai
On this
T.1
mp
3. Šai svē - tā nak - tī,
3. in this ho - ly night,
T.2
p
3. Šai svē - tā nak - tī,
3. On this ho - ly night,
Šai
On this
B.1
mp
3. svē - tā nak - tī,
3. in this ho - ly night,
B.2
p
3. Šai svē - tā nak - tī,
3. On this ho - ly night,
Šai
On this

26
cits ci - tu at - kal mī - ļo,
each loves the oth - er,
svē - tā nak - tī,
ho - ly night,
cits ci - tu at - kal mī - ļo,
each loves the oth -
svē - tā nak - tī,
ho - ly night,
cits ci - tu at - kal mī - ļo,
each loves the oth - er,
mp
svē - tā nak - tī,
ho - ly night,
Šai
On this
cits ci - tu at - kal mī - ļo,
each loves the oth -
svē - tā nak - tī,
ho - ly night,

29
p
Šai svē - tā nak - tī cits ci -
On this ho - ly night_ each_
p
nak - tī,
ho - ly night,
- er,
cits ci -
each
p
svē - tā nak - tī,
ho - ly night,
p
Šai svē - tā nak - tī cits ci -
On this ho - ly night_ each_
svē - tā nak - tī, šai svē - tā nak - tī,
ho - ly night, in this ho - ly night,
B.1
- er,
cits ci -
each
B.2
div.
Šai svē - tā nak - tī, svē - tā nak - tī,
On this ho - ly night, ho - ly night,
Šai svē - tā nak - tī, svē - tā nak - tī,
On this ho - ly night, in this ho - ly night,

32
mf
-tu at - kal mī - ļo.
loves the oth - er.
4. Šī nakts ir de - bess
4. On this night the gates of
p
at - kal mī - ļo.
the oth - er.
-tu at - kal mī - ļo.
loves the oth - - er.
4. ir de - bess
4. the gates of
at - kal mī - ļo.
each loves the oth - - - er.

35
f
vār-tus at - vē-ru - si, Pār ze - mes tum-su dedz tā zvaig-žņu lo -
hea - ven_ o - pen, A - bove earth's dark-ness arc___ the___ burn - ing
f
vār - tus at - vē - ru - si, ze - mes tum - su___ zvaig-žņu lo -
hea - ven o - - pen, A - bove earth's dark-ness arc the burn-ing
f
vār - tus at - vē - ru- si, ze - mes tum - su zvaig-žņu lo -
hea - ven o - - pen, A - bove earth's dark-ness arc the burn-ing
f
vār-tus at - vē-ru - si, Pār ze - mes tum-su dedz tā zvaig-žņu lo -
hea - ven_ o - pen, A - bove earth's dark-ness arc___ the___ burn - ing
f
vār - tus at - vē - ru - si, ze - mes tum - su___ zvaig-žņu lo -
hea - ven o - - pen, A - bove earth's dark-ness arc the burn-ing
f
vār - tus vē-ru - si, ze - mes tum - su zvaig-žņu lo -
hea - ven o - pen, A - bove earth's dark-ness arc the burn-ing

39
p
- ku. Un nak - tī šai uz ka tra gal - vu klu - si Dievs svē-tot uz-liek sa - vu
stars, And soft - ly on each per-son's head this night, The Lord in bless-ing lays his
p
- ku. Un nak - tī gal - vu klu - si Dievs uz - liek
stars, And on each per - son's head, The Lord in
p
- ku. Un nak - tī klu - si Dievs uz - liek
stars, each per - son's head, The Lord in
p
- ku. gal - vu klu - si
stars, each head,
43
rit.
pp
mī - ļo ro - ku. ro - ku.
lov - ing hand. bless - ing.
pp
sa - vu mī - ļo ro - ku. Dievs uz-liek sa - vu mī - ļo ro - ku.
bless-ing lays his lov - ing hand, the Lord in bless - ing lays his lov-ing hand.
pp
sa - vu mī - ļo ro - ku. Dievs uz-liek sa - vu mī - ļo ro - ku.
bless-ing lays his lov-ing hand, The Lord in bless-ing lays his lov - ing hand.
mf
pp
Dievs svē-tot uz-liek sa - vu mī - ļo ro - ku.
The Lord in bless-ing lays his lov - ing hand.
pp
Dievs uz - liek sa - vu mī - ļo ro - ku.
The Lord in bless-ing lays his hand.
rit.

O come, all ye faithful

(Adeste, fideles)

tr. F. Oakeley,
W.T. Brooke
and others

words and melody by
J.F. Wade (*c.* 1711–1786)
verses 6 & 7 arr. Stephen Cleobury

Note: Verses 1-5 may be sung by unison voices and organ, S.A.T.B. voices and organ, or voices unaccompanied as desired.
Note for the congregation: in the refrain to verses 1-6, the first two phrases are sung by upper voices only, with the lower voices joining for the third phrase. This is essential in verse 6. Verse 7 may be sung throughout by everyone.
Verses 3-5 may be omitted. The harmonies used for verses 1-5 are from *The English Hymnal.*

3. See how the shepherds,
   Summoned to his cradle,
Leaving their flocks, draw nigh with lowly fear;
   We too will thither
   Bend our joyful footsteps:
      O come, etc.

4. Lo! star-led chieftains,
   Magi, Christ adoring,
Offer him incense, gold, and myrrh;
   We to the Christ Child
   Bring our hearts' oblations:
      O come, etc.

5. Child, for us sinners
   Poor and in the manger,
Fain we embrace thee, with awe and love;
   Who would not love thee,
   Loving us so dearly?
      O come, etc.

* 6. Sing, choirs of angels
   Sing in exultation,
Sing, all ye citizens of heav'n above;
   Glory to God
   In the highest:
      O come, etc.

7. Yea, Lord, we greet thee,
   Born this happy morning,
Jesus, to thee be glory giv'n;
   Word of the Father
   Now in flesh appearing:
      O come, etc.

* Words of v.6 & 7 are included here for use of the congregation. For a full choral version of verse 6, see overleaf.

21
SOPRANO 1
6. Sing, choirs of an - gels, Sing in ex - ul - ta - tion, Sing, all ye
SOPRANO 2
6. Sing, choirs of an - gels, Sing in ex - ul - ta - tion, Sing, all ye
ALTO
6. Sing, choirs of an - gels, Sing in ex - ul - ta - tion, Sing, all ye
TENOR/BASS
6. Sing, choirs of an - gels, Sing in ex - ul - ta - tion, Sing, all ye
26
ci - ti - zens of heav'n a - bove; Glo - ry to God in
ci - ti - zens of heav'n a - bove; Glo - ry to God
ci - ti - zens of heav'n a - bove; Glo - ry to God
ci - ti - zens of heav'n a - bove; Glo - ry to God

31

the high - est: O come let us a - dore him, let us a -

in the high - est: O come let us a - dore him, O come let us a -

in the high - est: O come let us a - dore him, O come let us a -

in the high - est:

36

dore him, O come let us a - dore him, Christ the Lord.

- dore him, O come let us a - dore him, Christ the Lord.

dore him, O come let us a - dore him, Christ the Lord.

O come let us a - dore him, Christ the Lord.

41
ALL VOICES
7. Yea, Lord, we greet thee, Born this hap-py morn - ing, Je - su, to
46
thee be glo - ry giv'n; Word of the Fa - ther,
51
Now in flesh ap - pear - ing: O come let us a - dore him, O come let us a -
56
-dore him, O come let us a - dore him, Christ the Lord!

for Stephen Cleobury and the Choir of King's College, Cambridge

The shepherd's carol

Bob Chilcott
(b. 1955)

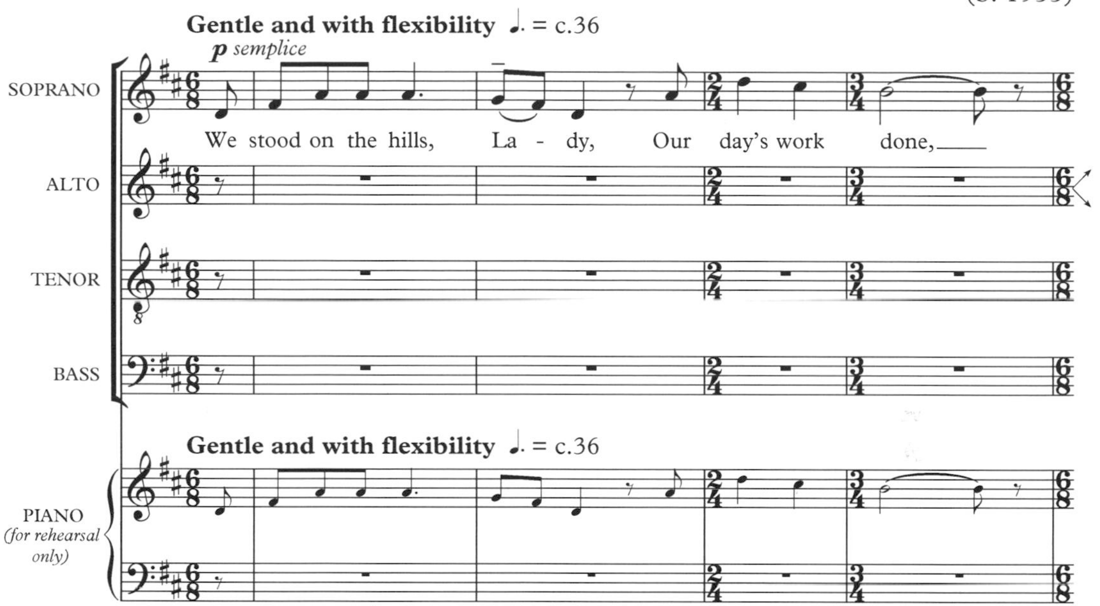

5

Watch-ing the frost-ed mea-dows That win-ter had won.

ALTO 1 *pp*

Calm,

ALTO 2 *pp*

Calm, calm,

9
SOPRANO 1
pp
Calm,
calm,
SOPRANO 2
pp
Calm, calm,
calm,
A.1
calm,
calm,
calm,
A.2
calm,
calm,
TENOR
p
The even-ing was calm, La - dy, The air so
13
Si - lence more love - ly than mu - sic
calm,
Si - lence more love - ly than mu - sic
Si - lence, si - - - lence,
calm,
Si - lence,
still,
pp
Si - lence more love - ly than mu - sic
BASS 1
pp
Si - - - lence,
BASS 2
pp
Si - - - lence,
si -

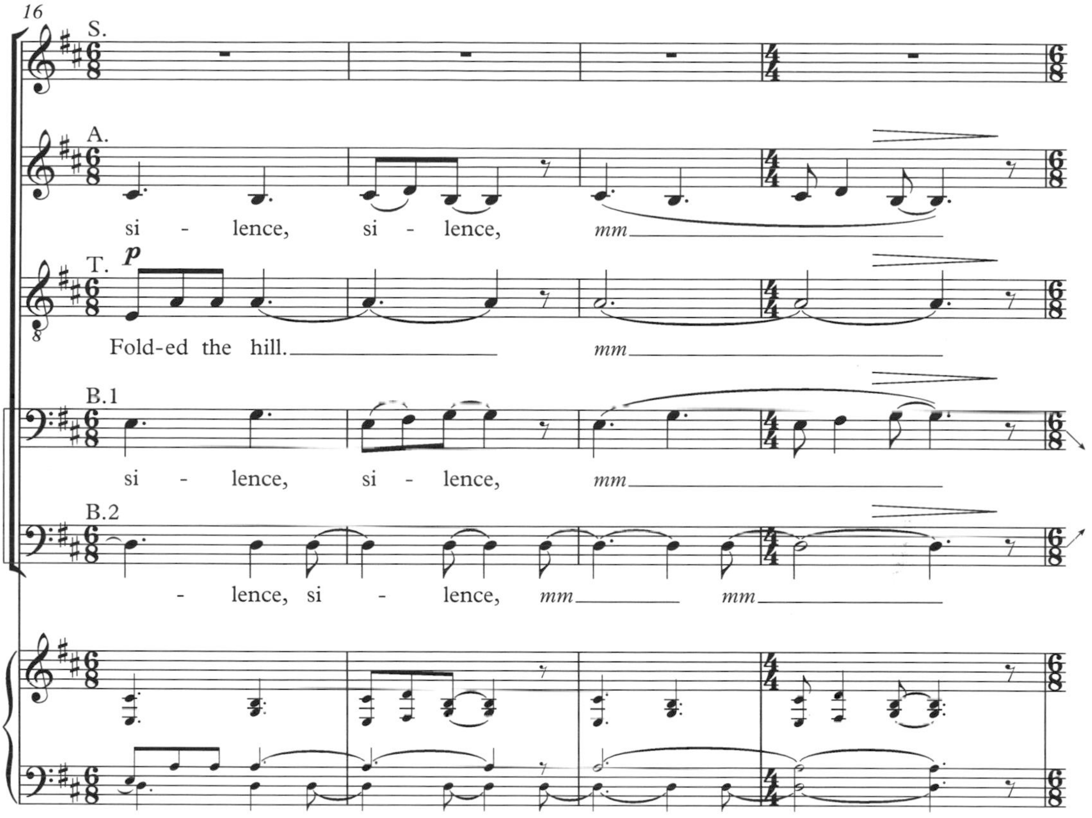
16
S.
A.
si - lence, si - lence, mm
T.
p
Fold-ed the hill. mm
B.1
si - lence, si - lence, mm
B.2
- lence, si - lence, mm mm

20
p
There was a star, La - dy, Shone in the night,
p
There was a star, La - dy, Shone in the night,
p
There was a star, La - dy, Shone in the night,
p
There a star shone

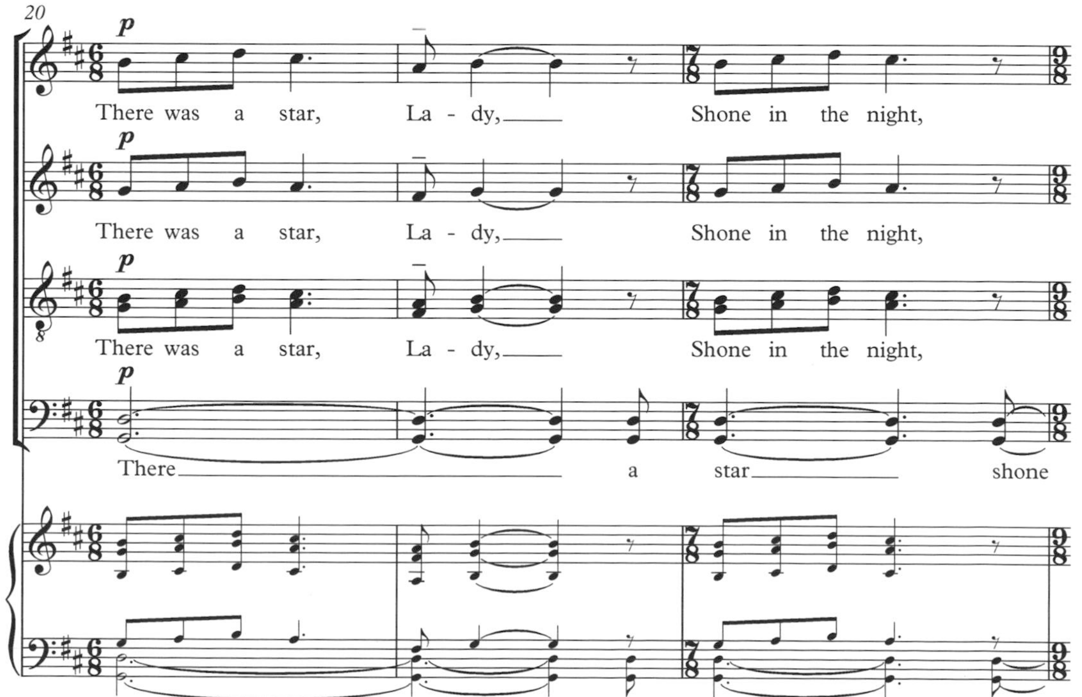

23

mf f ff appass.

Lar-ger than Ve-nus it was and bright, so__ bright. Oh, a voice from the sky,

Lar-ger than Ve-nus it was and bright, so__ bright. Oh, a voice from the sky,

Lar-ger than Ve-nus it was and bright, so__ bright. Oh, a voice from the sky,

__________ and bright, so__ bright. Oh, a voice from the sky,

27

p

La - dy,__ It__ seemed__ to us then__ Of God__

La - dy,__ It__ seemed__ to us then__ Of God__

La - dy,__ It__ seemed__ to us then__ Tell-ing of God be-ing

La - dy,__ It__ seemed__ to us then__ God__ be-ing

31
p
— being born — in the world of men. —
pp
— being born — La - dy, La - dy, — mm —
pp
born — La - dy, La - dy, — mm —
B.1
pp
born — La - dy, La - dy, — mm —
B.2
pp
born — La - dy, La - dy, — mm — mm
35
p semplice
And so we have come, La - dy, Our day's work

39
p
done, Our love, our hopes, our - selves we give to your son.
Love, our - selves La - dy,
Our love, our hopes, our - selves La - dy,
Love, our - selves La - dy,
Love, our - selves La - dy, La-
pp
43
rit.
La - dy, mm
- dy, mm mm
mm

Silent night

(2009 setting)

Joseph Mohr (1792–1848)
tr. anon.

Franz Gruber (1787–1863)
arr. Stephen Cleobury

* The keyboard introduction is optional, as are the links between the verses.

10

Ho - ly in - fant so ten - der and mild, Sleep in hea - ven - ly peace,____

__ Ho - ly__ in - fant so ten - der and mild,______ Sleep in hea - ven - ly peace,____ sleep_

__ Ho - ly__ in - fant so ten - der and mild,______ Sleep in hea - ven - ly peace,____ sleep_

p

Sleep in peace,______

14

sleep_ in hea - ven - ly peace.

____ in hea - ven - ly peace.

____ in hea - ven - ly__ peace.

__ in peace.

Organ

p

Ped.

19
p
2. Si - lent night, ho - ly night, Shep - herds first saw the sight: Glo
mp
2. Si - lent night, ho - ly night, Shep-herds first saw the sight:
p
2. Si - lent night, ho - ly night, Shep - herds first saw the sight: Glo
rehearsal only
23
p
Heav'n - ly hosts sing Al - le - lu - ia:
- ries stream from heav'n a - far, Heav'n - ly hosts sing Al - le - lu - ia:
Glo - ries stream from hea - ven a - far, Heav'n - ly hosts sing Al - le - lu - ia:
- ries stream from heav'n a - far, a - far.

27

Christ the Sav-iour is born, Christ the Sa-viour is born.

Christ the Sav-iour is born, Christ the Sa-viour is born.

Christ the Sav-iour is born, Christ the Sav-iour is born.

Christ is born, Christ is born.

Organ

p

Ped.

32

p

3. Si - lent night, ho - ly night, Son of God,

pp

3. Si - lent, ho - ly night, Son of

p

3. Si - lent night, ho - ly night, Son of God,

pp

3. Si - lent, ho - ly night, Son of

pp

3. Si - lent, ho - ly night, Son of

rehearsal only

37
poco cresc.
love's pure light; Ra-diance beams from thy ho - ly face, With the dawn of re-
poco cresc.
God, love's pure light; Ra - diance beams from thy ho - ly face, With re - deem - ing
poco cresc.
love's pure light; Ra-diance beams from thy ho - ly face, With the dawn of re-
poco cresc.
God, love's light; Ra - diance beams from thy ho - ly face, With re -
poco cresc.
God, love's pure light; Ra - diance beams from thy ho - ly face, With re -
41
mf
dim.
p
pp
-deem - ing grace, Je - sus, Lord, at thy birth, Je - sus, Lord, at thy birth.
grace, Je - sus, Lord, at thy birth, Lord, at thy birth.
-deem - ing grace, Je - sus, Lord, at thy birth, Je - sus, Lord, at thy birth.
-deem - ing grace, Je - sus, Lord, at thy birth, Je - sus, at thy birth.
-deem - ing grace, Je - sus, Lord, at thy birth, at thy birth.

for Zerlina

Sleep, little Jesus, sleep

English translation
by Anna Kaspszyk

trad. Polish
arr. Roxanna Panufnik (b.1968)

* Small notes for rehearsal only.

Lul-laj-że Je-zu-niu = *Lu-lay-zhe Ye-zu-nyu*

a = m<u>a</u>ster
e = w<u>e</u>t, s<u>e</u>t
u = tr<u>u</u>th
y = <u>y</u>es
zh = as in French: <u>j</u>alousie, <u>j</u>our

[1] Notwithstanding the comma, avoid any break here.

[1] Avoid any break (as in bar 24).

27
mp
com-fort you with her lul - la - by.
com-fort you with her lul - la - by.
com-fort you with her lul - la - by.
p
Lu - laj - że mm
loo - leye - je
mm
32
p
ah ah
Look down from Hea-ven all o - ver this earth,
mm ah ah
ah ah
ah ah ah

*small notes desirable but not compulsory!

43
Je - sus, hush,[1] don't you cry, Ma - ry will
Je - sus, hush,[1] don't you cry, Ma - ry will
lu - laj, lu - laj, Je - zu - niu,
loo - leye, loo - leye, Ye - zoo - nyoo,
lu - laj, lu - laj, Je - zu - niu,
loo - leye, loo - leye, Ye - zoo - nyoo,
lu - laj, lu - laj, Je - zu - niu,
loo - leye, loo - leye, Ye - zoo - nyoo,
47
com-fort you with her lul - la - by. Sleep, lit-tle Lord
com-fort you with her lul - la - by. Sleep, lit-tle Lord
ah Sleep, lit-tle Lord
ah Sleep, lit-tle Lord
ah Sleep, lit-tle Lord
mf

[1] As before.

* spoken/whispered

[1] As before.

to Olivia

Suo gân

Welsh traditional
arr. Stephen Cleobury

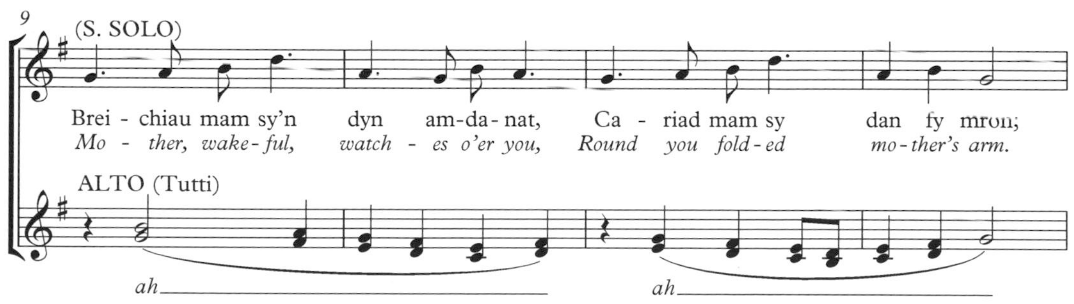

[1] The dynamic is *piano* throughout.

17
S. SOLO
Hu - na'n da-wel, an - nwyl blen-tyn, Hu - na'n fwyn ar fron dy fam.
Sleep, my ba-by, sleep and fear not, Sleep you sweet-ly on my breast.
ALTO
ah

21

25
TENOR SOLO
2. Hu - na'n da-wel, he - no, hu - na, Hu - na'n fwyn, y tlws ei lun;
2. Lul - la, lul-la, sweet - ly slum-ber, Mo - ther's trea-sure, slum - ber deep;

29
(T. SOLO)
Pam yr wyt yn awr yn gwe-nu, Gwe - nu'n di-rion yn dy hun?
Lul - la, lul-la, now you're smil-ing, Smil - ing, dear one, through your sleep.
BASS
ah
ah

33
T. TUTTI
Ai an-gy-lion fry sy'n gwe-nu, Ar - nat ti yn gwe-nu'n llon,
Say, are an-gels bend - ing o'er you, Smil - ing down from heav'n a - bove?

37
T. SOLO
Ti - thau'n gwe-nu'n ôl dan hu- no, Hu - no'n da - wel ar fy mron?
Is that heav'n-ly smile your an- swer, Love from dream-land an-swering love?
(BASS)
ah

41

45
SOPRANO
3. Paid ag of - ni, dim ond dei-len Gu - ra, gu - ra ar y ddôr;
3. Hush, my trea- sure, 'tis a leaf-let Beat - ing, beat-ing on the door;
ALTO
3. Paid ag of - ni, dim ond dei - len Gu - ra, gu - ra ar y ddôr;
3. Hush, my trea - sure, 'tis a leaf - let Beat- ing, beat - ing on the door;
TENOR
3. Paid ag of - ni, dim ond dei - len Gu - ra, gu - ra ar y ddôr;
3. Hush, my trea - sure, 'tis a leaf - let Beat- ing, beat - ing on the door;
BASS
3. Paid ag of - ni, dim ond dei - len Gu - ra, gu - ra ar y ddôr;
3. Hush, my trea - sure, 'tis a leaf - let Beat- ing, beat - ing on the door;
(rehearsal only)
49
Paid ag of-ni, ton fach u-nig Su - a, su-a ar lan y môr;
Hush, my pret- ty, 'tis the rip-ple Lap - ping, lap-ping on the shore.
Paid ag of - ni, ton fach u - nig Su - a, su - a ar lan y môr;
Hush, my pret - ty, 'tis the rip - ple Lap - ping, lap - ping on the shore.
Paid ag of - ni, ton fach u-nig Su - a, su - a ar lan y môr;
Hush, my pret - ty, 'tis the rip-ple Lap - ping, lap - ping on the shore.
Paid ag of - ni, ton fach u - nig Su - a, su - a ar lan y môr;
Hush, my pret - ty, 'tis the rip - ple Lap - ping, lap - ping on the shore.

53

S. TUTTI
Hu - na blen- tyn, nid oes y - ma Ddim i ro - ddi i ti fraw;
Mo - ther wat- ches, nought can harm you, An - gel war-ders ga - ther nigh;
(Man.)

57

S. SOLO
Gwe - na'n da-wel yn fy myn-wes Ar yr eng-yl gwy-nion draw.
Bless - ed an-gels, bend - ing o'er you, Sing your lul-la, lul - la - by.
ALTO
ah

61

Commissioned by King's College Cambridge
for the Festival of Nine Lessons and Carols, Christmas Eve 2000

The three Kings

Dorothy L. Sayers (1893–1957) — Jonathan Dove (b.1959)

15
(S. Solo 1)
mp
With dole - ful bal-lads on his tongue,
(S. Solo 2)
mp
With dole - ful bal-lads on his tongue,
pp
p
-low la lay, Ah O ba-
pp
p
-low la lay Ah O ba-
p poco
la lay Ba -
p poco
la lay Ba -
22
S.1 [Solo 1 tacet]
cresc.
poco f
-low, ba-low la lay, He came bear-ing a branch of myrrh Than
S.2 [Solo 2 tacet]
cresc.
-low, ba-low la lay, He came bear-ing a branch of
A.
-low, ba-low la lay,
T.
p
- low la lay, Ah
B.
- low la lay,

29
S. SOLO 1
mp
Than which no gall is
S. SOLO 2
mp
Than which no
S.1
which no gall is bit-ter-er,
S.2
poco f
myrrh Than which no gall is bit-ter-er,
A.1
mp
Ah
A.2
mp
Ah
T.1
pp
Ah
T.2
pp
Ah
B.

35
[col Tutti]
bit-ter-er,
[col Tutti]
gall is bit-ter-er,
p
O ba - low, ba - low la lay,
pp
p
Ah
O ba - low, ba - low la lay,
pp
p
Ah
O ba - low, ba - low la lay,
p
Ba - low, la lay,
p
Ba - low, la lay,
p
Ba - low, la lay,

41
S.1
p
Gifts for a ba - by King, O.
S.2
pp
Ah
A.1
p
Gifts for a ba - by King, O.
A.2
pp
Ah
T.
p
O ba - low, ba - low la
B.
p
O ba - low, ba - low la
A little faster ♩ = 120
48
f
The se - cond king was a man in prime, O ba - low, ba - low la
f
Ba - low la lay, O ba - low, ba - low la
lay, Ba - low la lay, Ba - low la
lay, Ba - low la lay, Ba - low la
A little faster ♩ = 120

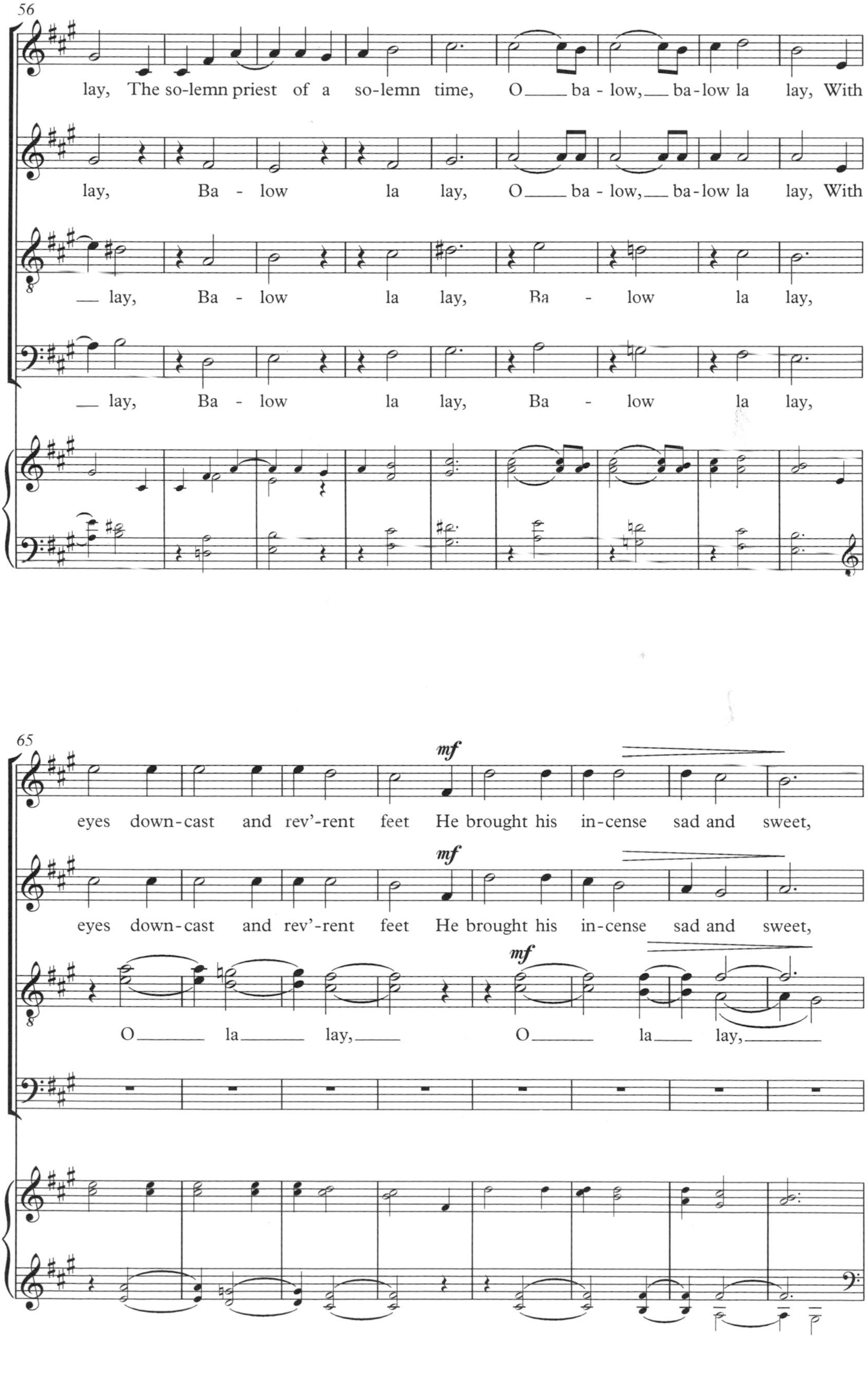

65

mf

eyes down-cast and rev'rent feet He brought his in-cense sad and sweet,

mf

eyes down-cast and rev'rent feet He brought his in-cense sad and sweet,

mf

O ___ la ___ lay, ___ O ___ la ___ lay, ___

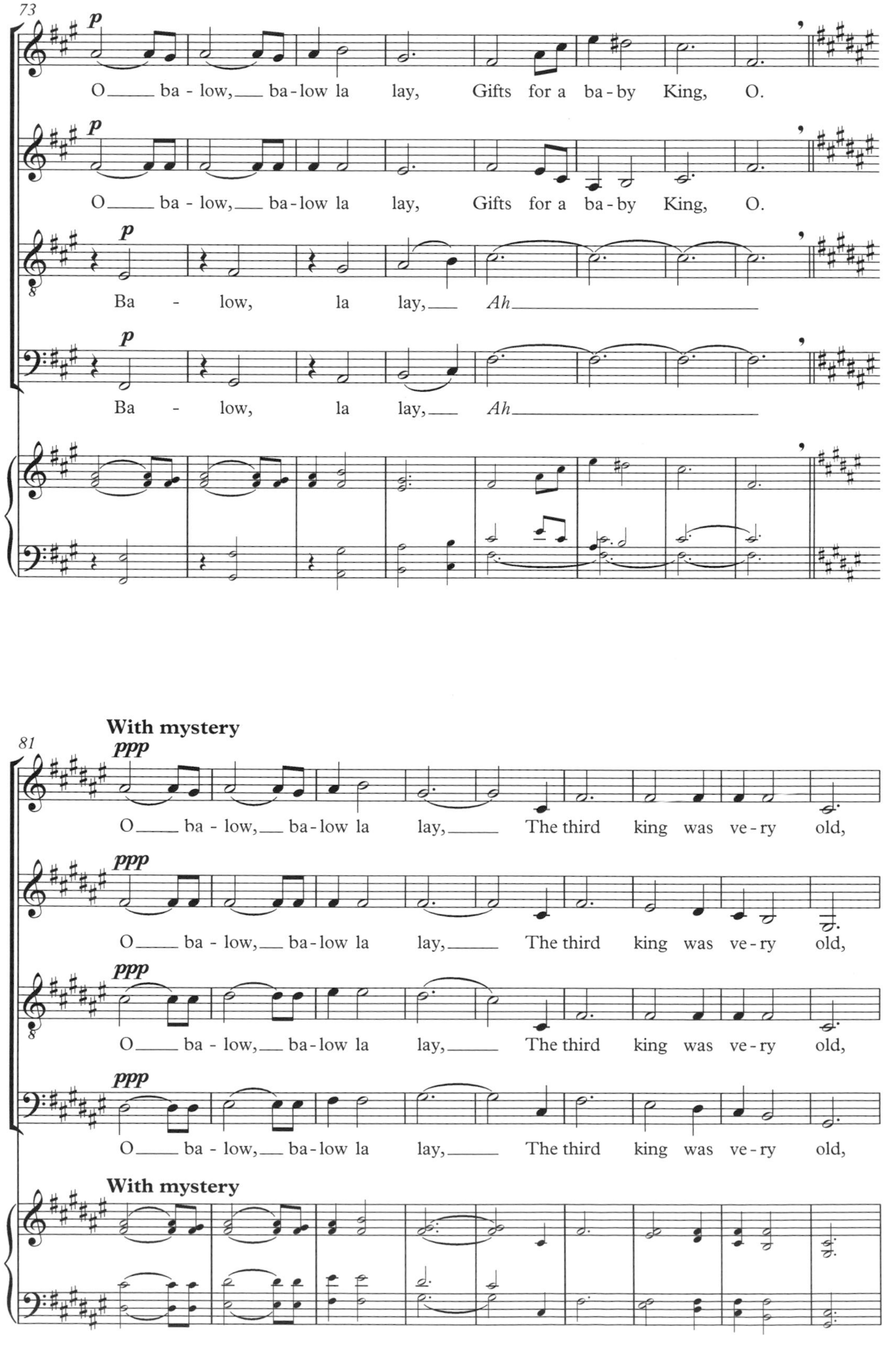

With mystery

81

ppp

O ba - low, ba-low la lay, The third king was ve-ry old,

ppp

O ba - low, ba-low la lay, The third king was ve-ry old,

ppp

O ba - low, ba-low la lay, The third king was ve-ry old,

ppp

O ba - low, ba-low la lay, The third king was ve-ry old,

With mystery

98

Energetic

f O ba - low, ba - low la lay, *f sempre* Ma-ny a gaud

A.1 *f* O ba - low, ba - low la lay, *mp leggero* Ma-ny a gaud and a

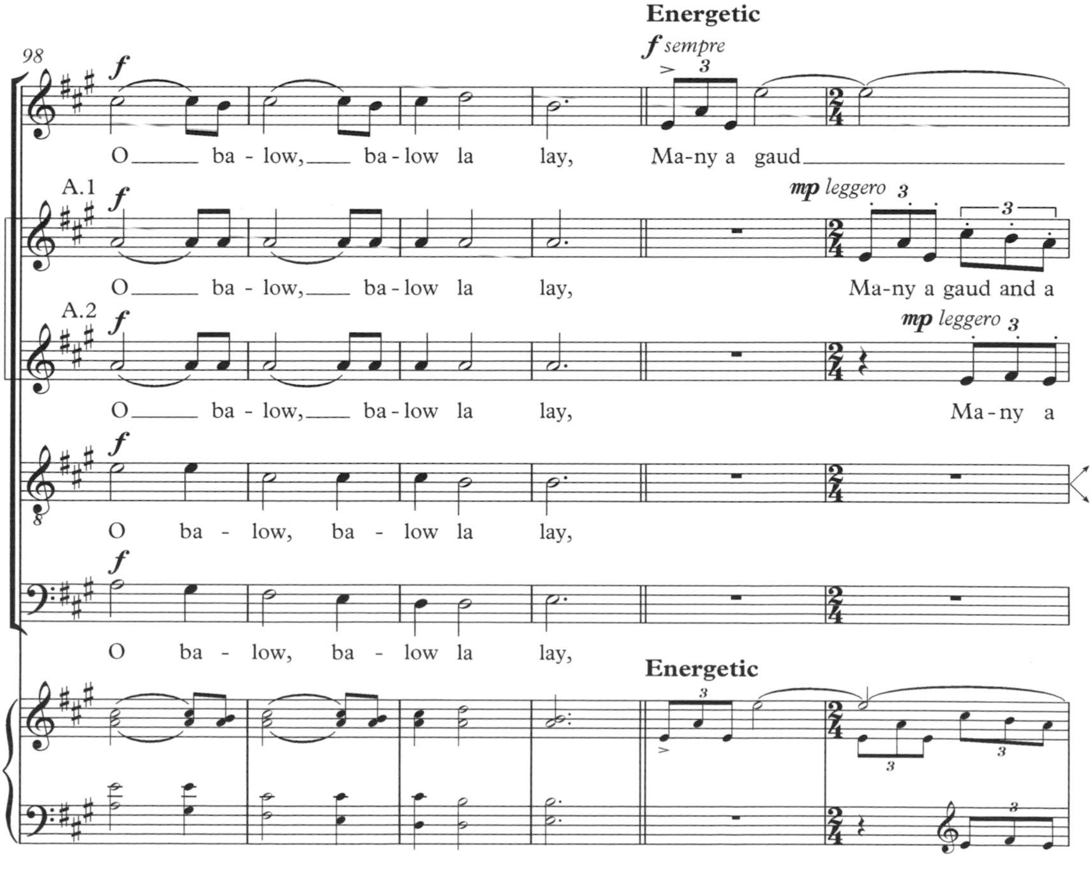

A.2 *f* O ba - low, ba - low la lay, *mp leggero* Ma-ny a

f O ba - low, ba - low la lay,

f O ba - low, ba - low la lay,

Energetic

104
and
glit-ter-ing toy
glit-ter-ing toy, ma - ny a gaud and a glit-ter-ing toy, ma - ny a gaud and a
gaud and a glit-ter-ing toy, ma - ny a gaud and a glit-ter-ing toy, ma - ny a
mp leggero
Ma - ny a gaud and a glit-ter-ing toy, ma - ny a gaud and a glit-ter-ing toy,
mp leggero
Ma - ny a gaud and a glit-ter-ing toy, ma - ny a gaud and a glit-ter-ing
108
S.1
S.2
mp
Ma - ny a gaud
glit - ter - ing toy, ma - ny a gaud and a glit - ter - ing toy,
gaud and a glit - ter - ing toy, ma - ny a gaud and a glit - ter - ing
ma - ny a gaud and a . . . ma - ny a gaud and a
toy, ma - ny a . . . ma - ny a

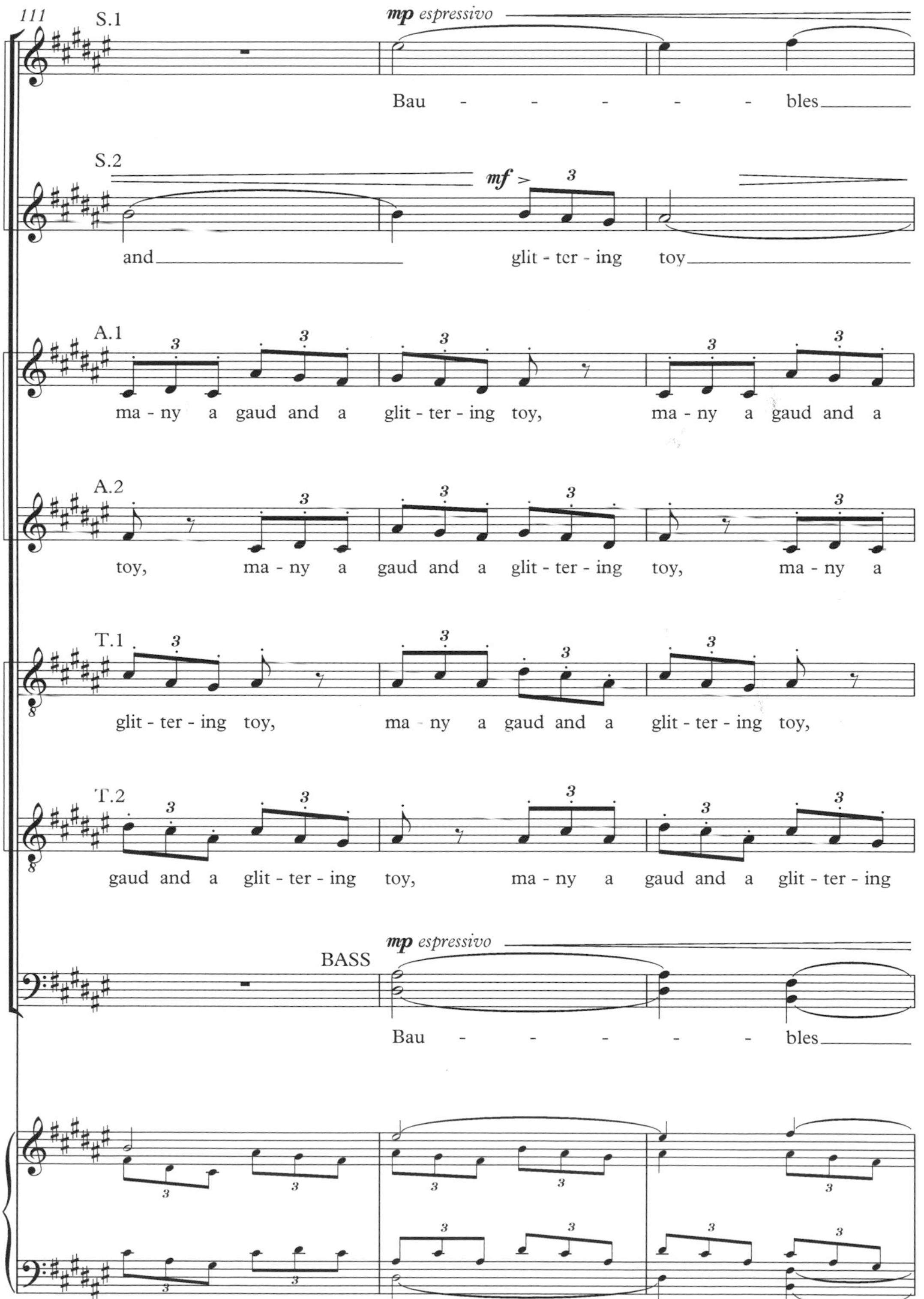
111
S.1
mp espressivo
Bau - - - - - bles
S.2
mf
and glit - ter - ing toy
A.1
ma - ny a gaud and a glit - ter - ing toy, ma - ny a gaud and a
A.2
toy, ma - ny a gaud and a glit - ter - ing toy, ma - ny a
T.1
glit - ter - ing toy, ma - ny a gaud and a glit - ter - ing toy,
T.2
gaud and a glit - ter - ing toy, ma - ny a gaud and a glit - ter - ing
BASS
mp espressivo
Bau - - - - - bles

114
poco f
brave
for a ba - -
for a ba - -
glit-ter-ing toy, ma-ny a gaud and a glit-ter-ing toy, ma-ny a gaud and a
gaud and a glit-ter-ing toy, ma - ny a gaud and a glit-ter-ing toy, ma - ny a
ma-ny a gaud and a glit-ter-ing toy, ma-ny a gaud and a glit-ter-ing toy,
toy, ma - ny a gaud and a glit-ter-ing toy, ma - ny a gaud and a glit-ter-ing
poco f
brave
for a ba - -

118
S.
- by boy:
A.1
glit - ter - ing toy, ma - ny a gaud and a glit - ter - ing toy,
A.2
gaud and a glit - ter - ing toy, ma - ny a gaud and a glit - ter - ing toy,
T.1
ma - ny a gaud and a glit - ter - ing toy, ma - ny a glit - ter - ing toy,
T.2
toy, ma - ny a gaud and a glit - ter - ing toy,
B.
- by boy.
121
O ba - low ba - low la lay
O ba - low ba - low la lay
O ba - low, ba - low ba - low la lay
O ba - low, ba - low ba - low la lay

124
f
Ma-ny a gaud and glit-ter-ing toy Ma-ny a gaud and glit-ter-ing toy
f
Ma-ny a gaud and glit-ter-ing toy Ma-ny a gaud and glit-ter-ing toy
f
Ma-ny a gaud and glit-ter-ing toy Ma-ny a gaud and glit-ter-ing toy
f
Ma-ny a gaud and glit-ter-ing toy Ma-ny a gaud and glit-ter-ing
128
With fervour
ff
O ba - low, ba - low la lay, O ba - low, ba-
ff
O ba - low, ba - low la lay, O ba - low, ba-
ff
toy, ba-low, ba-low, ba-low la lay, O ba - low, ba -
ff
toy, ba-low, ba-low, ba-low la lay, O ba - low, ba -
With fervour

133

A little slower

mp

-low la lay____ O____ ba - low,____ ba-low la lay____

mp

-low la lay____ O____ ba - low,____ ba-low la lay____

mp

-low la lay____ O ba - low, ba - low la lay____

mp

-low la lay____ O ba - low, ba - low la lay____

A little slower

141

Still slower

pp

O____ ba - low,____ ba-low la lay, Gifts for a ba-by King, O.

pp

O____ ba - low,____ ba-low la lay, Gifts for a ba-by King, O.

pp

Ba - low la____ lay, *Ah*____

pp

Ba - low la____ lay, *Ah*____

Still slower

for Stephen Cleobury and the Choir of King's College, Cambridge

What sweeter music

Robert Herrick*
(1591-1674)

John Rutter
(b.1945)

* slightly abridged and altered.

Version with string orchestra accompaniment available from OUP.

13
Poco meno mosso
night, fly hence a - way, And give the ho - nour to this day That sees De -
night, fly hence a - way, And give the ho - nour to this day That sees De -
Poco meno mosso
17
poco rit.
a tempo
(♩ = 66)
pp
That sees De - cem - ber turn'd to May.
pp
That sees De - cem - ber turn'd to May.
p pp mp cantabile
- cem - ber turn'd to May, That sees De - cem - ber turn'd to May. Why does the
p pp mp cantabile
- cem - ber turn'd to May, That sees De - cem - ber turn'd to May. Why does the
poco rit.
a tempo
p
mp
21
3
chill - ing win-ter's morn Smile, like a field be - set with corn? Or smell like a
3
chill - ing win-ter's morn Smile, like a field be - set with corn? Or smell like a
Ped.

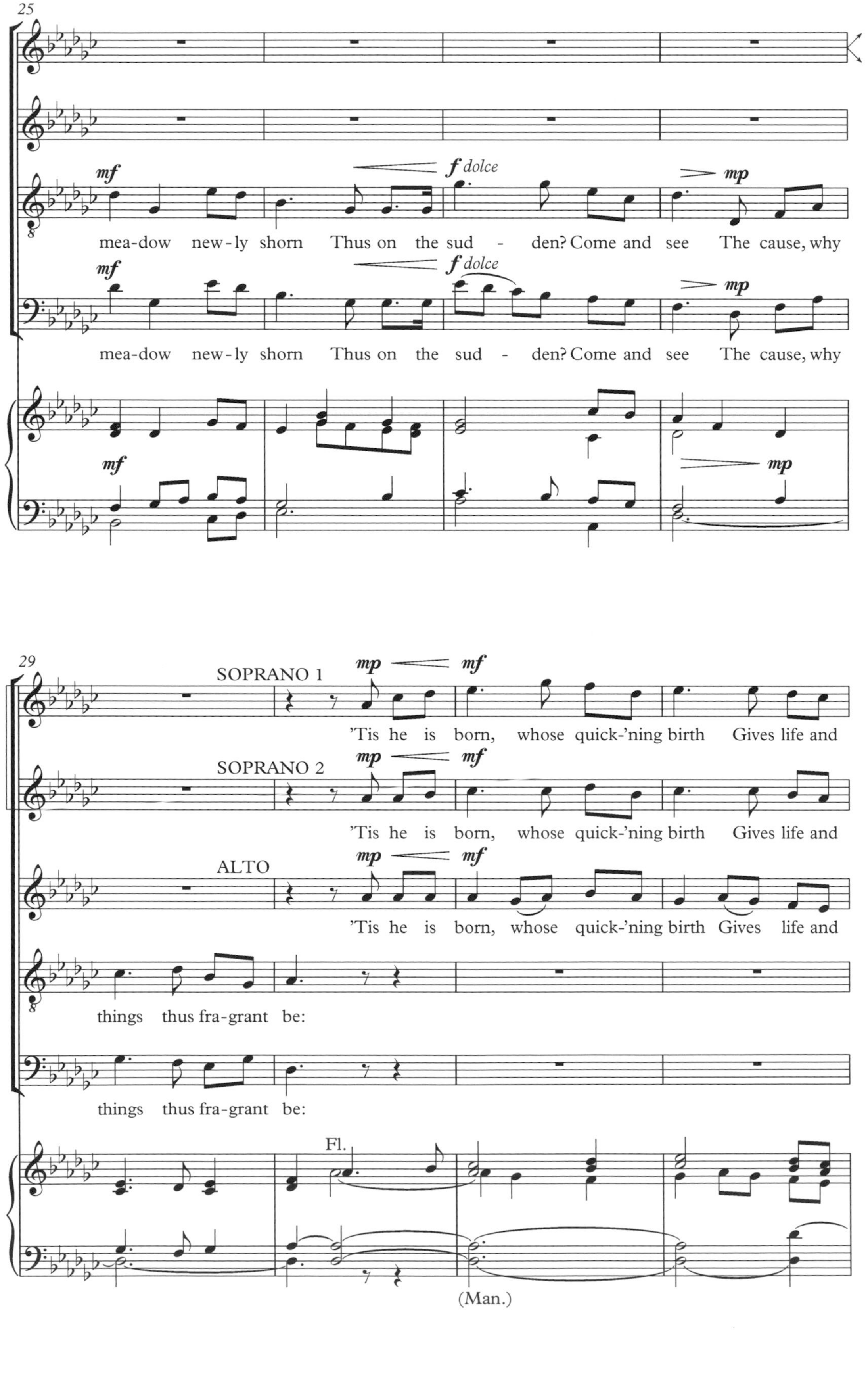

29

SOPRANO 1

mp mf

'Tis he is born, whose quick-'ning birth Gives life and

SOPRANO 2

mp mf

'Tis he is born, whose quick-'ning birth Gives life and

ALTO

mp mf

'Tis he is born, whose quick-'ning birth Gives life and

things thus fra-grant be:

things thus fra-grant be:

Fl.

(Man.)

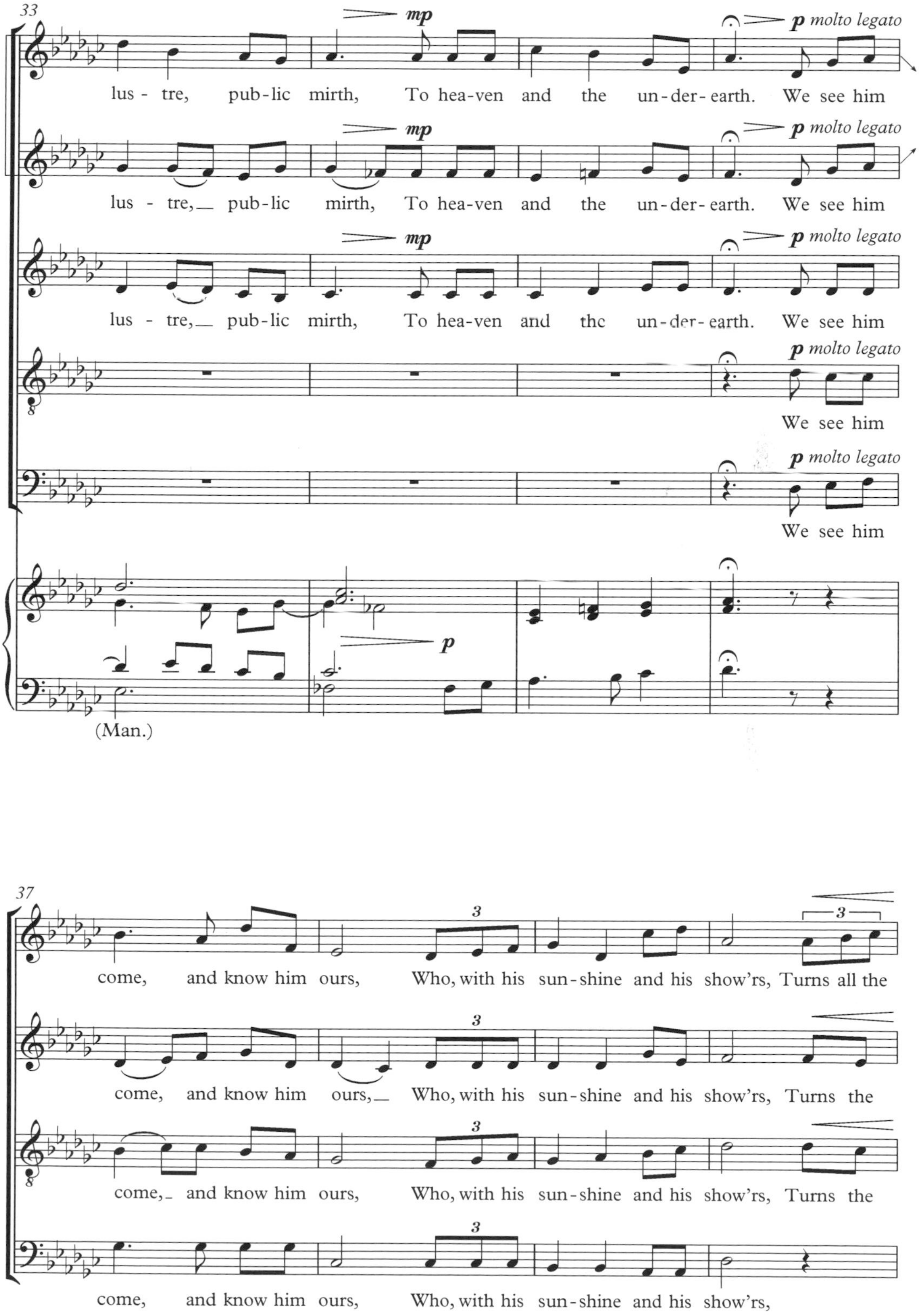

33

mp — p molto legato

lus - tre, pub-lic mirth, To hea-ven and the un-der-earth. We see him

lus - tre, pub-lic mirth, To hea-ven and the un-der-earth. We see him

lus - tre, pub-lic mirth, To hea-ven and the un-der-earth. We see him

We see him

We see him

p

(Man.)

41
mp
mf
p
pp
pa - tient ground to flow'rs, turns all the pa - tient ground to flow'rs. The
pa - tient ground to flow'rs, turns all the pa - tient ground to flow'rs. The
pa - tient ground to flow'rs, turns all the pa - tient ground to flow'rs. The
turns all the ground to flow'rs.
45
dar-ling of the world is come, And fit it is, we find a room To
dar-ling of the world is come, And fit it is, we find a room To
(pp)
dar - ling of the world is come, we find a
49
wel-come him, to wel-come him.
wel-come him, to wel-come him.
room to wel-come him. The no-bler part of all the house here, is the
cresc.
The no-bler part of all the house here, is the
(Man.)
Ped.

53
Which we will give him; and be - queath This
Which we will give him; and be - queath This
heart, Which we will give him; and be - queath This
heart, Which we will give him; and be - queath This
56
hol - ly, and this i - vy wreath,
hol - ly, and this i - vy wreath,
hol - ly, and this i - vy wreath, To do him ho - nour; who's our
B.1
hol - ly, and this i - vy wreath, To do him ho - nour; who's our
B.2
hol - ly, and this i - vy wreath, To do him ho - nour; who's our
(Ped.)

59
mf
poco f
mf
p
And Lord of all this re - vel - ling.
King, And Lord of all this re - vel - ling.
King, And Lord of all this re - vel - ling.
King, And Lord of all this re - vel - ling.
pp molto dolce
(Ped.)
63
pp molto dolce
What sweet-er mu - sic can we bring Than a ca - rol, for to
What sweet-er mu - sic can we bring Than a ca - rol, for to
What sweet-er mu - sic can we bring Than a ca - rol, for to
What sweet-er mu - sic can we bring Than a ca - rol, for to

67

Poco meno mosso

mp **poco rit.** *p*

sing The birth of this our heav'n-ly King, the birth of

sing The birth of this our heav'n-ly King? *mm*

sing The birth of this our heav'n-ly King? *mm*

sing The birth of this our heav'n-ly King? *mm*

poco rit. **Poco meno mosso**

mp *dim.*

70

rit. **a tempo** *pp*

this our hea - ven - ly King.

rit. **a tempo** **rit.**

pp

(Ped.)

When Christ was born of Mary free

15th century

John Joubert (b.1927)

No. 4 of *Five Songs of Incarnation*, Op.163

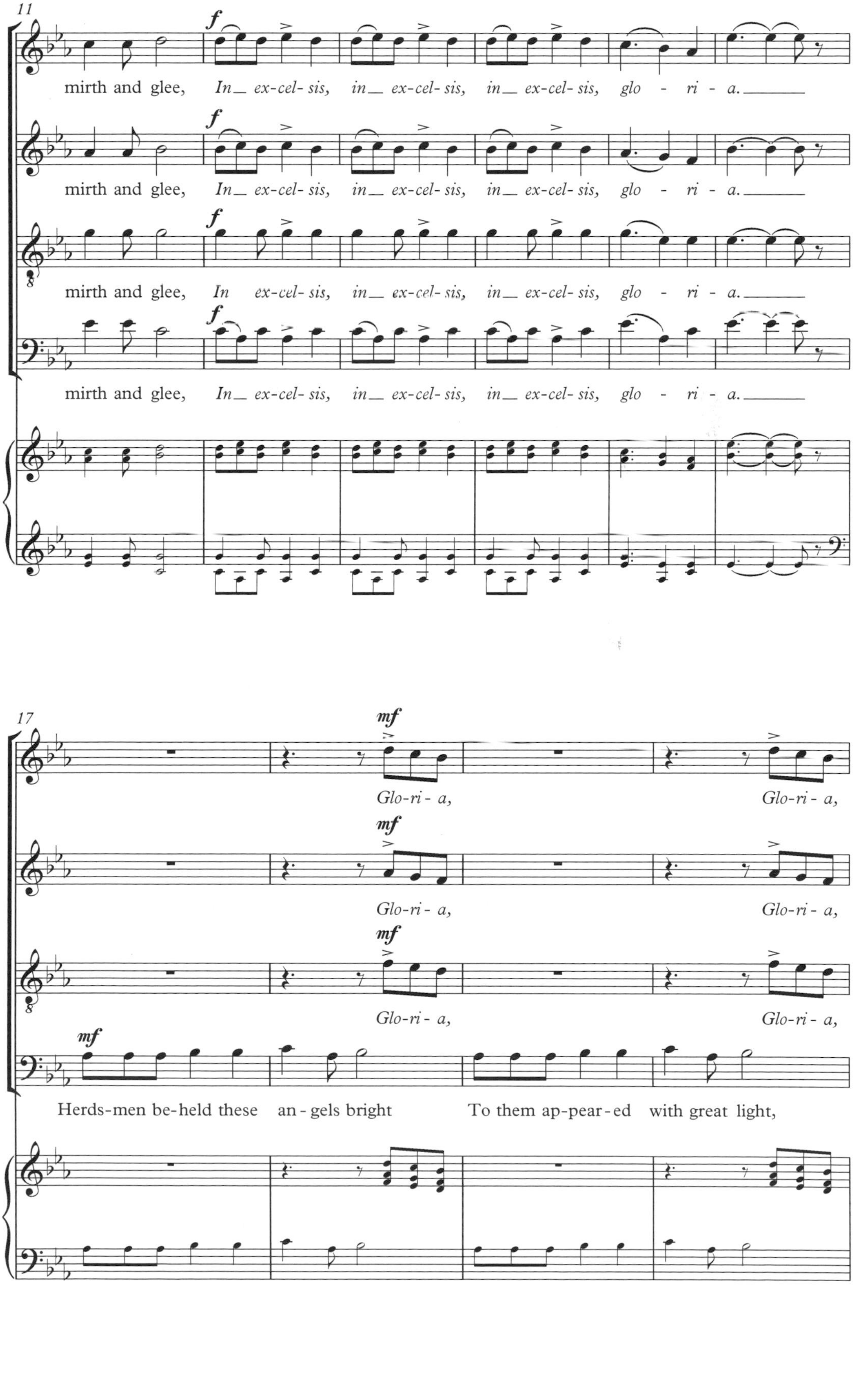

11

f

mirth and glee, *In — ex-cel- sis, in — ex-cel- sis, in — ex-cel- sis, glo - ri - a.* ———

mirth and glee, *In — ex-cel- sis, in — ex-cel- sis, in — ex-cel- sis, glo - ri - a.* ———

mirth and glee, *In ex-cel- sis, in — ex-cel- sis, in — ex-cel- sis, glo - ri - a.* ———

mirth and glee, *In — ex-cel- sis, in — ex-cel- sis, in — ex-cel- sis, glo - ri - a.* ———

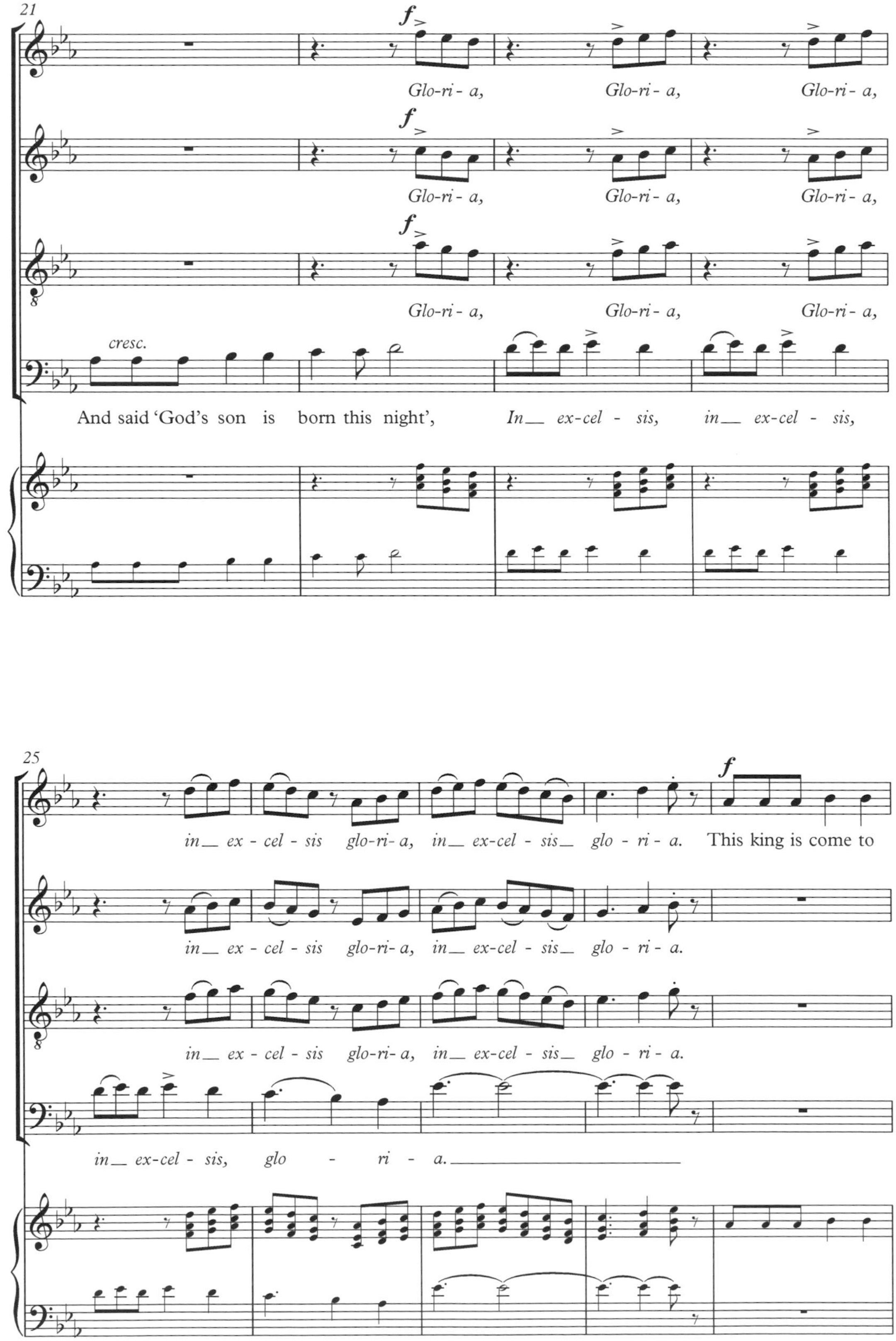

21

f

Glo-ri- a, Glo-ri- a, Glo-ri- a,

f

Glo-ri- a, Glo-ri- a, Glo-ri- a,

f

Glo-ri- a, Glo-ri- a, Glo-ri- a,

cresc.

And said 'God's son is born this night', *In__ ex-cel - sis, in__ ex-cel - sis,*

30
save his kind, In the scrip-ture as we find; There-fore this song have
Glo-ri - a, Glo-ri - a,
Glo-ri - a, Glo-ri - a,
Glo-ri - a, Glo-ri - a,

34
we in mind: In ex-cel - sis, in ex-cel - sis, in ex-cel - sis,
Glo-ri - a, Glo-ri - a, Glo-ri - a, in ex-
Glo-ri - a, Glo-ri - a, Glo-ri - a, in ex-
Glo-ri - a, Glo-ri - a, Glo-ri - a, in ex-

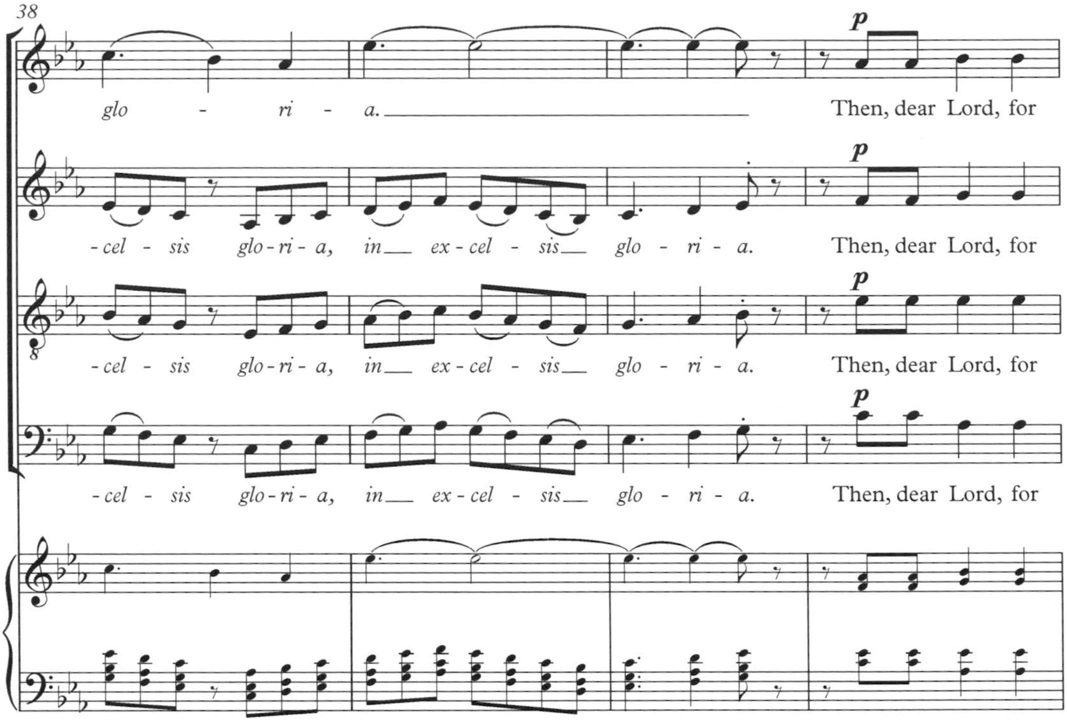
38
p
glo - ri - a.
Then, dear Lord, for
-cel - sis glo-ri-a, in ex-cel - sis glo - ri - a.
Then, dear Lord, for
-cel - sis glo-ri-a, in ex-cel - sis glo - ri - a.
Then, dear Lord, for
-cel - sis glo-ri-a, in ex-cel - sis glo - ri - a.
Then, dear Lord, for

42
cresc.
thy great grace, Grant us the bliss to see thy face, Where we may sing to
thy great grace, Grant us the bliss to see thy face, Where we may sing to
thy great grace, Grant us the bliss to see thy face, Where we may sing to
thy great grace, Grant us the bliss to see thy face, Where we may sing to

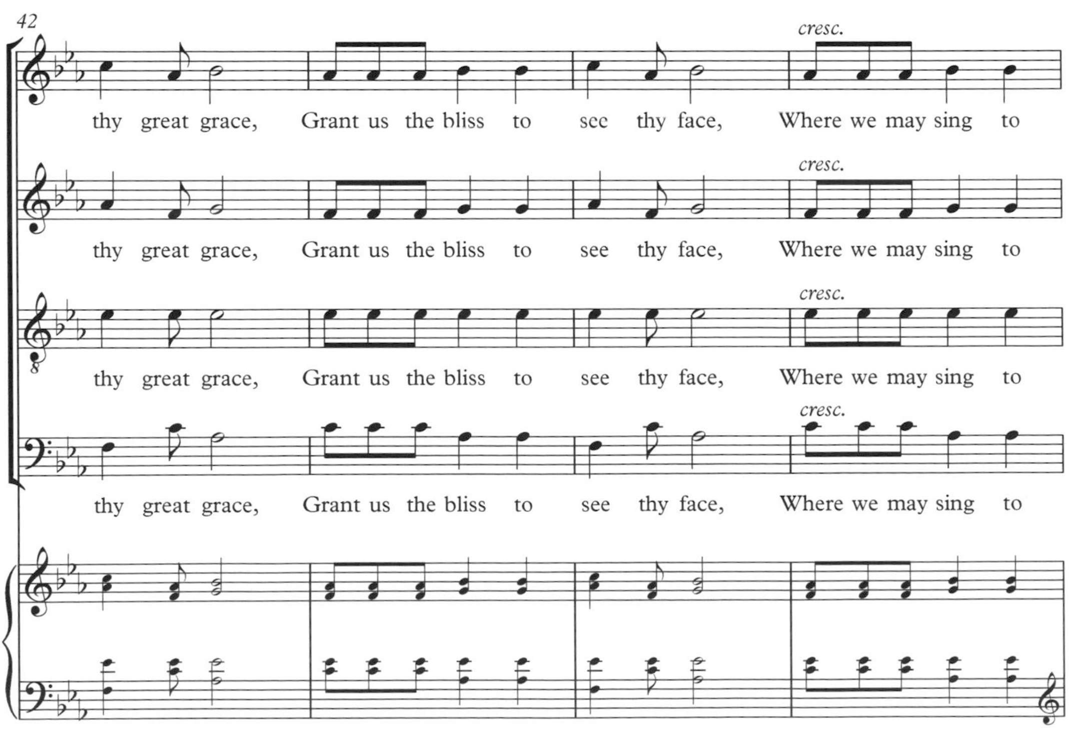

46

f

thy so-lace: *In — ex-cel-sis, in — ex-cel-sis, in — ex-cel-sis, glo - ri - a.*

thy *In — ex-cel-sis, in — ex-cel-sis, in — ex-cel-sis, glo - ri - a.*

thy *In ex-cel-sis, in — ex-cel-sis, in — ex-cel-sis, glo - ri - a.*

thy so-lace: *In — ex-cel-sis, in — ex-cel-sis, in — ex-cel-sis, glo - ri - a.*

Poco lento: maestoso

52

ff

Chris-to pa-re-mus can - ti - ca, — In — ex-cel - sis glo - ri - a.

Chris-to pa-re-mus can - ti - ca, — In — ex-cel - sis glo - ri - a.

Chris-to pa-re-mus can - ti - ca, — In — ex-cel - sis glo - ri - a.

Chris-to pa-re-mus can - ti - ca, — In — ex-cel - sis glo - ri - a.

Poco lento: maestoso

While shepherds watched their flocks by night

Nahum Tate (1652–1715)

after Christopher Tye
verse 6 arr. Stephen Cleobury

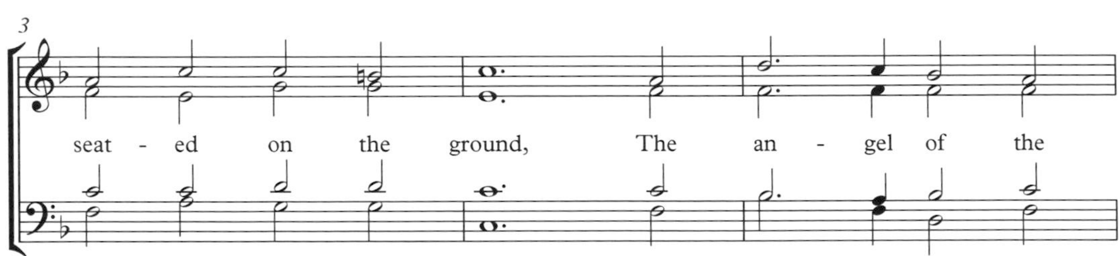

2. 'Fear not,' said he (for mighty dread
Had seized their troubled mind);
'Glad tidings of great joy I bring
To you and all mankind.

3. 'To you in David's town this day
Is born of David's line
A Saviour, who is Christ the Lord;
And this shall be the sign:

4. 'The heavenly Babe you there shall find
To human view displayed,
All meanly wrapped in swathing bands,
And in a manger laid.'

5. Thus spake the Seraph; and forthwith
Appeared a shining throng
Of Angels praising God, who thus
Addressed their joyful song:

[CONGREGATION: SING TENOR LINE.]

Hark! the herald angels sing

Charles Wesley (1707–88)
and others

Felix Mendelssohn (1809–47)
verse 3 arr. Stephen Cleobury

21
SOPRANO
3. Hail the heav'n-born Prince of Peace! Hail the Sun of
ALTO
3. Hail the heav'n - born Prince of Peace! Hail the Sun of
TENOR
3. Hail the heav'n - born Prince of Peace! Hail the Sun of
BASS
3. Hail the heav'n-born Prince of Peace! Hail the Sun of
24
Right-eous-ness! Light and Life to all he brings, Ris'n with heal-ing
Right-eous - ness! Light and Life to all he brings, Ris'n with heal - ing
Right-eous - ness! Light and Life to all he brings, Ris'n with heal-ing
Right-eous - ness! Light and Life to all he brings, Ris'n with heal-ing

28
in his wings; Mild he lays his glo - ry by, Born that man no
in his wings; Mild he lays his glo - ry by, Born that man no
in his wings; Mild he lays his glo - ry by, Born that man no
in his wings; Mild he lays his glo - ry by, Born that man no
32
more may die, Born to raise the sons of earth,
more may die, Born to raise the sons of earth, Born
more may die, Born to raise the sons of earth,
more may die, Born to raise the sons of earth,

35
Born to give them second birth. Hark! the herald angels sing
to give them second birth. Hark the herald angels sing
Born to give them second birth. Hark! the herald angels sing
Born to give them second birth. Hark! the herald angels sing
39
Glory to the newborn King.
Glory to the newborn King.
Glory to the newborn King.
Glory to the newborn King.

Readings and repertoire for A Festival of Nine Lessons and Carols

Bold denotes congregational

Processional hymn

Once in royal David's city — Gauntlett & Mann, arr. Cleobury

BIDDING PRAYER

Beloved in Christ, be it this Christmas Eve [*or* at this Christmas-tide] our care and delight to prepare ourselves to hear again the message of the Angels, and in heart and mind to go even unto Bethlehem and see this thing which is come to pass, and the Babe lying in a manger.

Therefore let us hear again from the Holy Scripture the tale of the loving purposes of GOD from the first days of our sin unto the glorious Redemption brought us by this Holy Child: and let us make this (Chapel, dedicated to His pure and lowly Mother,) glad with our carols of praise.

But first, because this of all things would rejoice His heart, let us pray to Him for the needs of the whole world, and all His people; for peace upon the earth He came to save; for love and unity within the one Church He did build; for brotherhood and goodwill amongst all men, (and especially within the dominions of our sovereign lady Queen Elizabeth, within this University and Town of Cambridge, and the two royal and religious Foundations of King Henry VI here and at Eton).

And particularly at this time let us remember before Him the poor, the cold, the hungry, the oppressed; the sick and them that mourn; the lonely and the unloved; the aged and the little children; all those who know not the Lord Jesus, or who love Him not, or who by sin have grieved his heart of love.

Lastly let us remember before Him them who rejoice with us, but upon another shore and in a greater light, that multitude which no man can number, whose hope was in the Word made flesh, and with whom, in this Lord Jesus, we for evermore are one.

These prayers and praises let us humbly offer up to the Throne of Heaven, in the words which Christ himself hath taught us:

Our Father, which [who] art in heaven, Hallowed be thy Name. Thy kingdom come. Thy will be done, in [on] earth as it is in heaven. Give us this day our daily bread. And forgive us our trespasses, As we forgive them that [those who] trespass against us. And lead us not into temptation; But deliver us from evil: For thine is the kingdom, the power, and the glory, For ever and ever. Amen.

The Almighty God bless us with His grace: Christ give us the joys of everlasting life: and unto the fellowship of the citizens above may the King of Angels bring us all. *Amen.*

Then shall the congregation sit.

The readers of the lessons should be appointed after a definite order; in a cathedral, for instance, from chorister to bishop.
Each reader should announce the lesson by the descriptive sentence attached to it. At the end of the lesson, the reader should pause and say: Thanks be to God.

O little town of Bethlehem (I)	arr. Vaughan Williams, desc. Stephen Cleobury
Alleluya, a new work is come on hand	Peter Wishart
The birthday of thy King	Peter Sculthorpe
Nowel	Richard Rodney Bennett
O little town of Bethlehem (II)	Henry Walford Davies
Of the Father's heart begotten	arr. Stephen Cleobury
On Christmas night all Christians sing	arr. Philip Ledger
The truth sent from above	arr. Vaughan Williams
What sweeter music	John Rutter

FIRST LESSON: *God tells sinful Adam that he has lost the life of Paradise and that his seed will bruise the serpent's head.*	Genesis 3:8-15, 17-19
Adam lay ybounden	Philip Ledger
Jesus Christ the apple tree	Elizabeth Poston
Morning song for the Christ Child	Peter Sculthorpe
On Christmas night all Christians sing	arr. Philip Ledger
The truth sent from above	arr. Vaughan Williams
SECOND LESSON: *God promises to faithful Abraham that in his seed shall all the nations of the earth be blessed.*	Genesis 22: 15-18
I saw three ships come sailing in	arr. Simon Preston
I wonder as I wander	Carl Rütti
Šai svētā naktī	arr. Stephen Cleobury
THIRD LESSON: *The prophet foretells the coming of the Saviour.*	Isaiah 9: 2, 6-7
A tender shoot	Otto Goldschmidt
Alleluya, a new work is come on hand	Peter Wishart
God rest you merry, gentlemen	arr. David Willcocks
Illuminare, Jerusalem	Judith Weir
It came upon the midnight clear	arr. Stephen Cleobury
O little town of Bethlehem (I)	arr. Vaughan Williams, desc. Stephen Cleobury
O little town of Bethlehem (II)	Henry Walford Davies
On Christmas night all Christians sing	arr. Philip Ledger
FOURTH LESSON: *The peace that Christ will bring is foreshown.*	Isaiah 11: 1-4 (to 'meek of the earth'), 6-9
A great and mighty wonder	Praetorius arr. James Whitbourn
A tender shoot	Otto Goldschmidt
Alleluya, a new work is come on hand	Peter Wishart
The Lamb	John Tavener
FIFTH LESSON: *The angel Gabriel salutes the Blessed Virgin Mary.*	St Luke 1: 26-35, 38
Bogoroditse Dyevo	Arvo Pärt
Benedicamus Domino	Peter Warlock
I sing of a maiden	Patrick Hadley
SIXTH LESSON: *St Luke tells of the birth of Jesus.*	St Luke 2: 1, 3-7
A virgin most pure	arr. Stephen Cleobury
The birthday of thy King	Peter Sculthorpe
Christo paremus cantica	Diana Burrell
I wonder as I wander	Carl Rütti
The Infant King	arr. David Willcocks
Myn lyking	R.R. Terry
Silent night	Franz Gruber arr. Stephen Cleobury
Sleep, little Jesus, sleep	arr. Roxanna Panufnik
Suo gân	arr. Stephen Cleobury
What sweeter music	John Rutter

SEVENTH LESSON:
The shepherds go to the manger. St Luke 2: 8-16

Away in a manger	John Tavener
Christo paremus cantica	Diana Burrell
God rest you merry, gentlemen	arr. David Willcocks
I wonder as I wander	Carl Rütti
In wintertime	Lennox Berkeley
Infant holy, infant lowly	arr. Stephen Cleobury
The shepherd's carol	Bob Chilcott
Silent night	Franz Gruber arr. Stephen Cleobury
When Christ was born of Mary free	John Joubert
While shepherds watched their flocks by night	arr. Stephen Cleobury

EIGHTH LESSON:
The wise men are led by the star to Jesus. St Matthew 2: 1-11

Be merry	Stephen Cleobury
Illuminare, Jerusalem	Judith Weir
No small wonder	Paul Edwards
Noël nouvelet	arr. Stephen Jackson
The three Kings	Jonathan Dove

The congregation shall stand for the ninth lesson.

NINTH LESSON:
St John unfolds the great mystery of the Incarnation. St John 1: 1-14

Love came down at Christmas	R.O. Morris
O come, all ye faithful	J.F. Wade arr. Stephen Cleobury

Minister: The Lord be with you.
People: And with thy spirit.
Then all shall kneel.
Minister: Let us pray.

THE COLLECT FOR CHRISTMAS EVE
(from the 1928 *Book of Common Prayer*)

O God, who makest us glad with the yearly remembrance of the birth of thy only Son, Jesus Christ: Grant that as we joyfully receive him for our redeemer, so we may with sure confidence behold him, when he shall come to be our judge; who liveth and reigneth with thee and the Holy Spirit, one God, world without end. *Amen.*

or THE COLLECT FOR CHRISTMAS DAY

Almighty God, who hast given us thy only-begotten Son to take our nature upon him, and as at this time to be born of a pure Virgin: Grant that we being regenerate, and made thy children by adoption and grace, may daily be renewed by thy Holy Spirit; through the same our Lord Jesus Christ, who liveth and reigneth with thee and the same Spirit, ever one God, world without end. *Amen.*

THE BLESSING
May he who by his Incarnation gathered into one things earthly and heavenly, fill you with the sweetness of inward peace and goodwill; and the blessing of God Almighty, the Father, the Son, and the Holy Ghost, be upon you and remain with you always. *Amen.*

Hark! the herald angels sing arr. Stephen Cleobury

Good King Wenceslas has never been used in the Festival of Nine Lessons and Carols. It has, however, been used in the TV 'Carols from King's', as it has occasionally fitted with a reading.